THIS DARK SHELTERING FOREST

ALSO BY MAGI NAMS

in the *Cry of the Kiwi* trilogy:

Once a Land of Birds

Tang of the Tasman Sea
Available June 2015

ABOUT THE AUTHOR

MAGI NAMS studied zoology at the University of Alberta and high arctic plant ecology at Dalhousie University before turning to writing. She is passionate about exploring the natural world and has published dozens of nature articles in the children's magazine *Ranger Rick*. The ten months she and her family lived in New Zealand became the subject of her *Cry of the Kiwi* trilogy. She lives in Nova Scotia, Canada, and is working on her next book, *Red Continent*, about a year of birding, bushwalking, and exploring in Australia. Visit her website at **www.maginams.ca**.

AUTHOR'S NOTE

This is the second book of the *Cry of the Kiwi* trilogy. The first book, *Once a Land of Birds*, chronicles my family's first four months in New Zealand. We explore volcanic Banks Peninsula near Christchurch; Buller District's rain-swept, mountain-crowded valleys; Otago's rolling grasslands; the majestic Southern Alps near Queenstown; and the Canterbury Plain, with its immense, sheared hedges. My husband, Vilis, begins ecological research aimed at helping to rid New Zealand of stoats (public enemy number one of New Zealand birds). My sons, twelve-year-old Dainis [DINE-is], and nine-year-old Jānis [YAWN-is], and I dive into New Zealand history and immerse ourselves in the educational opportunity of a lifetime. We all embrace life in small-town New Zealand, delve into Kiwi culture, and embark on an outdoor adventure odyssey that has us scrambling up volcanoes, hiking over wind-blasted pastures, and trail riding in the shadow of the Southern Alps.

This Dark Sheltering Forest carries on from where *Once a Land of Birds* leaves off and chronicles my family's North Island adventures. The people, places, and events in this book are real. Some individuals' names and identifying characteristics have been changed to protect their privacy.

THIS DARK SHELTERING FOREST

Cry of the Kiwi:
A Family's New Zealand Adventure

Book 2: North Island

MAGI NAMS

All rights reserved. No part of this book may be reproduced or distributed in print, audio, or electronic form by any means (including electronic, mechanical, graphic, photocopying, recording or otherwise) or by any information storage retrieval system without the prior written permission of the author. Permission is granted to use brief quotations in reviews. Please respect the author's rights and do not engage in electronic piracy of this copyrighted work.

Copyright © 2015 by Magi Nams. All rights reserved.

For more information, contact Magi Nams at **www.maginams.ca**

Library and Archives Canada Cataloguing in Publication

Nams, Magi, author
      Cry of the kiwi : a family's New Zealand adventure / Magi Nams

Includes bibliographical references and index.
Contents: Book 2. North Island. This dark sheltering forest
Issued in print and electronic formats.
ISBN 978-0-9937767-1-7 (bk. 2 : paperback).--ISBN 978-0-9937767-4-8 (bk. 2 : html).

      1. Nams, Magi--Travel--New Zealand. 2. New Zealand--Description and travel. 3. Natural history--New Zealand. 4. Ecology--New Zealand. 5. Home schooling. I. Title. II. Title: This dark sheltering forest.

DU413.N34 2015   919.304412   C2015-902223-1
                                                    C2015-902224-X

Editing by Pat Thomas
Cover and interior design by Magi Nams
Photography by Vilis, Magi, Dainis, and Jānis Nams
Map by Vilis and Magi Nams

Permission to quote brief passages from the following works is gratefully acknowledged:
New Zealand Geothermal Association website, on p. 68.
Penguin Books – *A History of New Zealand* by Keith Sinclair, on p. 119.
Department of Conservation interpretive sign, on p. 169.

If a permission has been inadvertently overlooked, the author and publisher apologizes and will be happy to make a correction.

FOR VILIS, DAINIS, AND JĀNIS

THE MEN OF MY HEART

CONTENTS

MAP

PREFACE

ACKNOWLEDGEMENTS

PROLOGUE   1

THIS DARK SHELTERING FOREST   5

GLOSSARY   179

REFERENCES   181

INDEX   186

OUR TRAVELS, DECEMBER 2000– JANUARY 2001

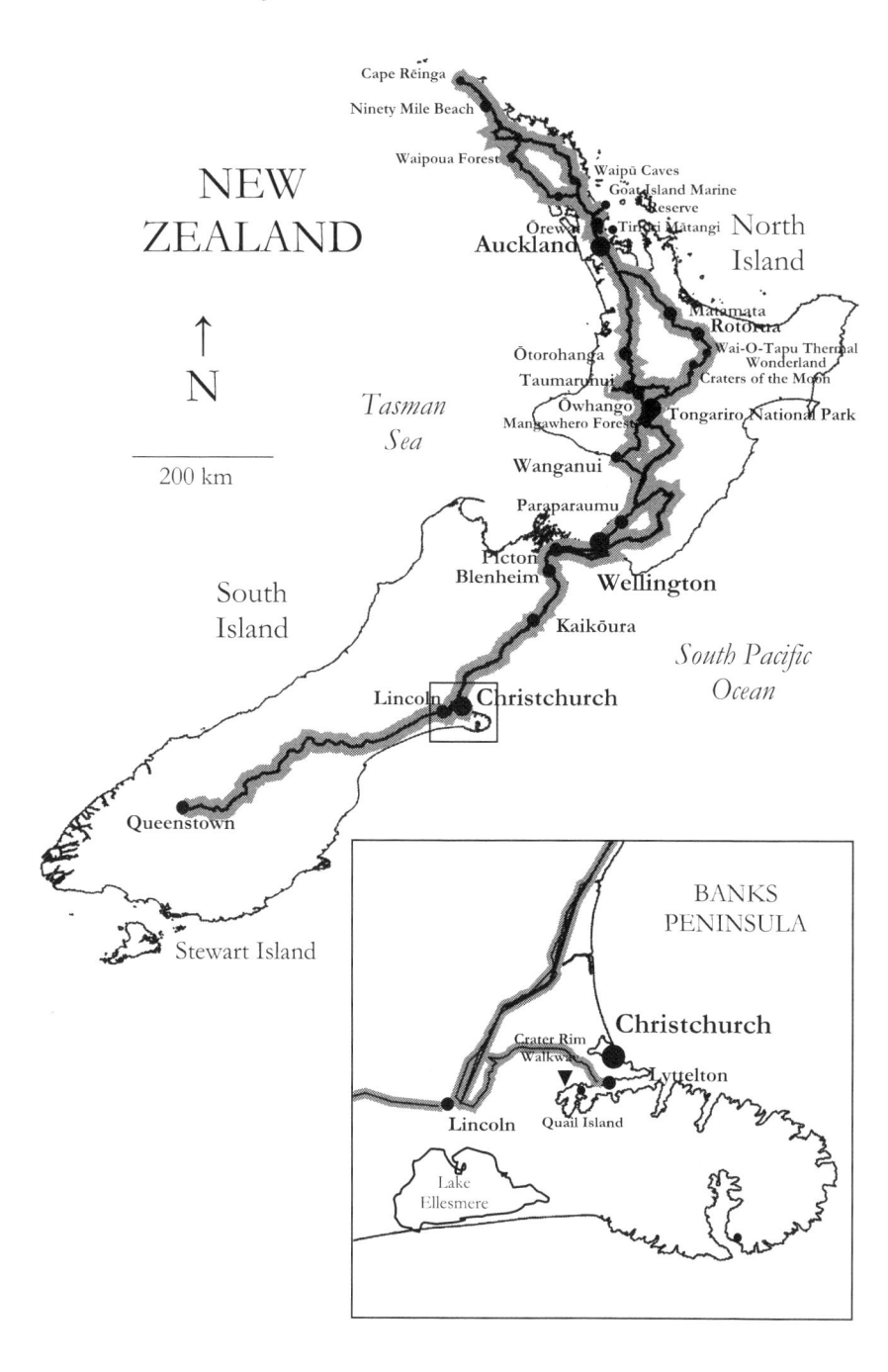

PREFACE

ALL MY life, I'd dreamed of travelling to far-away countries to hike through landscapes inhabited by exotic animals and plants I'd seen in *National Geographic* or on television. In the year 2000, my dream came true when my husband, two sons, and I left our home in rural Nova Scotia, Canada, and spent ten months in New Zealand.

Our sojourn on the far side of the world was our first extended absence from Canada. As we made our final preparations to travel, we were filled with excitement at the prospect of hiking on volcanoes and exploring tangled rainforests (maybe we'd even see a kiwi bird!) but we also had qualms. Would the tenant renting our house take good care of it? Would our cats remember us when we returned? Would we like New Zealand? Would the kids make friends? Would we be safe?

We didn't pack much to take with us: some clothes, a laptop, binoculars, skates, sleeping bags, and a box of school books. We arrived in New Zealand wide-eyed and unsure of what to expect. Ten months later we returned to Canada inspired and broadened in ways I'd never imagined. Our New Zealand adventure opened our eyes to the world and helped shape who we are.

The *Cry of the Kiwi* trilogy began as observations I scribbled in small notebooks during my family's travels and outdoor adventures in New Zealand, and entries in our homeschooling journal. While living there, I roughed out a few "NZ stories" intended for a private memoir. After our return to Canada, a persistent internal voice told me I should write more of our adventures and turn them into a book.

As happens in life, other responsibilities intruded, with the result that *Cry of the Kiwi* was fourteen years in the making and became one story in three parts: *Once a Land of Birds, This Dark Sheltering Forest,* and *Tang of the Tasman Sea.*

As our New Zealand adventure drew to a close in 2001, I realized that the heart of that country lay as much in its people as in its riveting landscapes and intriguing flora and fauna. Thank you, New Zealand, for the adventure of a lifetime. Perhaps my family's story will inspire others to go adventuring far from home.

Kia ora,
Magi Nams

ACKNOWLEDGEMENTS

WITHOUT THE assistance and encouragement of many people, this book would not be in your hands. Monica Graham offered insightful suggestions for an early draft and instilled in me the belief that my family adventure story could succeed. The diverse and thoughtful comments provided by beta readers Betty Hodgson, Leanne Erickson, Nikki Figueiredo, and Vilis Nams encouraged me and enabled me to polish an advanced draft. Editor Pat Thomas transformed my book dream into a clear and consistent manuscript and discerned that *Cry of the Kiwi* was really three books, not one.

In New Zealand, Christchurch City Libraries staff provided me with helpful contacts and answered numerous questions. Staff at the Māori Language Commission macronized Māori place names for me. Numerous Kiwis offered my family generous hospitality and friendship during our time in their beautiful country – my sincere gratitude to you all! Thanks also to the individuals who allowed me to include their true identities in my story, and special thanks to Andrea and Andy for giving us a home before we found a home.

Last but never least, loving thanks to my husband, Vilis, who supported me throughout this project and rescued me from numerous computer dilemmas. And hugs to my sons, Dainis and Jānis, who didn't balk at allowing me to share their roles in our New Zealand adventure with the world.

THIS DARK SHELTERING FOREST

PROLOGUE

August 9, 2000

ORANGE STREAKS flare against the night like a beckoning light at the end of the world. I stare through the window at waning darkness while my husband, Vilis, and sons, Dainis and Jānis, sleep onboard the Air New Zealand jet. A strip of cloud below the jet looks like thick smoke, tinged with the colour of ripe muskmelon. Through gaps in the cloud, I see steel-blue waves like beaten metal, and brown peaks like the humps of stampeding bison. A thrill runs through me. *This is it!* These are my first glimpses of Nieuw Zeeland (so named by Dutch geographers for their coastal province of Zeeland). To the Māori, whose ancestors arrived from Polynesia centuries before the Dutch explorer Abel Tasman sailed in search of a southern continent in 1642, this is Aotearoa, "Land of the Long White Cloud."[1]

At 5:00 a.m., a lingering darkness cloaks Auckland International Airport. Groggy from jetlag after flying half way around the world, my family trudges through New Zealand Customs. We're detained by a sniffer dog, a beagle who's detected the scent of fruit emanating from my daypack. If I had any fruit, it would have been a contravention of New Zealand's strict biosecurity regulations intended to prevent pests and diseases from entering the country,[2] however I ate the last dried apricot somewhere over the Pacific Ocean. We're released from the dog's inspection and follow directions that lead us through the airport and beyond its doors. The caress of warm air in the southern winter startles us.

"Look! There's a *palm* tree!" Jānis's voice is filled with

wonder.

Despite our weariness, the sight of those gracefully curved, exotic leaves sparks excitement in us. We're four Canadians 18 000 kilometres away from home (an old farm in Nova Scotia) where palm trees definitely do not grow outdoors!

This is why we came. This is why we left the familiarity of Nova Scotia for the newness of New Zealand. We had a need to explore a part of the world far away, to see new plants and animals and landscapes, to seek new adventures and feel new experiences jolt our senses and expand our horizons. For years, as a homeschooling parent, I'd wanted to live with my husband and kids in a foreign country. Such an adventure would be the ultimate fieldtrip. As the only ecologist on staff at the Nova Scotia Agricultural College, Vilis had for years looked forward to taking a leave to focus exclusively on his research, with no teaching responsibilities. When the New Zealand possibility arose, he and I leapt at the chance. And our sons? Jānis radiated excitement at the prospect of travel adventures. Dainis was torn between the contentment of remaining in Nova Scotia with his beloved home, friends, and LEGO, and the desire for new experiences.

Those new experiences start now, and it's Vilis's research that's made them possible. We've come to New Zealand because of an animal Kiwi conservationists wish didn't exist in their country: the stoat. A stoat is a kind of weasel. It's been declared public enemy number one of New Zealand's native birds,[3] particularly this country's national icon and unofficial symbol, the kiwi. You know the kiwi: dumpy and flightless, almost blind, and with a long beak like a poker. It's the reason New Zealanders are colloquially called "Kiwis." All five kiwi species face extinction, and stoats, which prey on kiwi chicks, are one of the main threats to kiwi survival.[4] This is where

Vilis, who has experience live-trapping and radio-tracking weasels and other predatory mammals in Canada, enters the picture. He'll assume a short-term position with Landcare Research, a government agency that studies and manages terrestrial ecosystems. His research will be aimed at helping to rid New Zealand of stoats.

As we stand in the warm Auckland darkness staring at a palm tree, I feel my family's horizons stretch. What adventures will the next ten-and-a-half months bring? For one of those months, Dainis, Jānis, and I will help Vilis live-trap and radio-track stoats in the Tongariro Forest Conservation Area on North Island, the northernmost half of this country. During the remainder of our sojourn, we'll be based near the Landcare Research branch in Lincoln, a township twenty kilometres southwest of Christchurch in the South Island province of Canterbury. There, as a family, we'll embark on a homeschooling and outdoor adventure odyssey intended to immerse us in New Zealand's history, culture, landscapes, flora, and fauna. As for me personally, I have three goals for my time in New Zealand: lots of hiking, lots of birding, and lots of writing. We've been fortunate to receive the travel and educational opportunity of a lifetime, and I plan to make the most of every minute…

THIS DARK SHELTERING FOREST

December 1, 2000

VILIS STEERS our 1985 Ford Sierra station wagon, the Blue Bomb, through the narrow Kawarau River Valley en route to Lincoln, 460 kilometres to the northeast. We've been exploring Otago and Queenstown for the past six days and are on our way home to the South Island province of Canterbury.

In the back seat, Dainis and Jānis read while we drive by paddocks holding red deer, sheep, and cattle. We also pass colourful clumps of blooming lupins and Scotch broom, both highly invasive plants introduced into New Zealand as ornamentals that subsequently went wildly astray.[5] Fields that appear turquoise-green in the distance turn out to be vineyards with colourful plastic tree protectors guarding the grape vines. Lombardi poplars, planted by a farmer, stand tall against the hills. Introduced wild roses grow as huge shrubs that cloak hillsides and infest pastures. The roses are yet another invasive species in a country struggling to control introduced plant and animal species that threaten native ecosystems.

It was one of these introduced species, the stoat, that brought my family to this country. In two weeks time, we'll head to North Island and the Department of Conservation's stoat research site at Ōwhango. There, Dainis, Jānis, and I will assist Vilis in his research aimed at determining how far juvenile stoats disperse. This is with a view to determining how large an area must be trapped free of stoats to keep it stoat-free, and thus safe for vulnerable flightless birds such as New Zealand's five kiwi species and its rare night parrot, the *kākāpō*.

At Cromwell, we begin a northward journey through hills and valleys that flank the Southern Alps' eastern foothills. On a road map, the short highway segment alongside Lake Dunstan is straight. However, north of the lake, the road squirms through uplands and dodges the toes of Lakes Pūkākī and Tekapō, which, like zigzaggy Lake Wakatipu beside Queenstown, were formed by glaciers tens of thousands of years ago.

SOUTH ISLAND'S GLACIATED LAKES

Lakes Wakatipu, Pūkākī, Tekapō, and eight other glaciated lakes resemble monstrous claw marks slashed from northwest to southeast across South Island's mountainous terrain. They include seven of New Zealand's ten largest lakes, including Lake Te Ānau, the country's second largest and the largest on South Island. Among these lakes are also the three deepest in the country: Lake Hauroko at 462 metres, Lake Manapōuri at 444 metres, and Lake Wakatipu at 380 metres. The glaciers clawed so deep that the beds of Lakes Manapōuri, Wakatipu, and Te Ānau lie below sea level.[6]

North of Cromwell, we're surrounded by dry beige hills and plateaus at the feet of the Dunstan Mountains. Their reflections create a multi-coloured mosaic of land and sky on Lake Dunstan's surface. Near Tarras, windbreaks of tall trees border flatland pastures. Beyond the town, the valley broadens into the wide, rolling agricultural landscape of the Lindis Valley. Here, sheep abound, and willows grow huge and lush along river courses.

With a curve in the road, we leave the valley and embark on a winding, rolling drive among hills as dry and thrusting as the Port Hills bordering Christchurch, or the tawny hills near Ranfurly, to the east in Otago. Within Lindis Pass Scenic Reserve, the road meanders through olive-brown grassland that carpets valleys and conical hills.

The open landscape reminds me of alpine tundra.

LINDIS PASS SCENIC RESERVE

Beyond the reserve, we drive across a flatter valley bordered by snow-capped peaks of the Barrier and Young Ranges to the west. The valley is traversed by the Ahuriri River, a tree-lined curve of beauty beside which I wish I could ride horses forever.

This valley is the southern margin of the Mackenzie Basin, known to South Islanders as "Mackenzie Country." The basin spreads northward between mountain ranges for a hundred kilometres and is New Zealand's largest inland depression. In the past, it provided quality grazing land for vast high-country sheep stations. Now, behind its dry, open beauty lies a sweeping trend toward desertification and another tale of New Zealand's war against invasive species, this time, rabbits.[7]

Unfortunately, it appears the rabbits are winning. We saw evidence of this at the closed Blackburn Mine near Mount Somers in October, where rabbit scat littered the dry hilltops, and where rabbits had pruned fiercely thorned gorse shrubs into the shapes of mushrooms.

> ### The War Against Rabbits
>
> Already battered as a result of unwise burning of native vegetation by both Māori (New Zealand's indigenous people) and Pākehā (Caucasian settlers) and then by sheep overgrazing, the Mackenzie Basin took an even bigger hit when European grey rabbits introduced to South Island in the mid-1800s rapidly multiplied, ravaging the semi-arid grasslands.[8]
>
> Farmers and government cullers shot rabbits, fenced them out, gassed them, and dropped poisoned carrots from airplanes. In 1887, 164 000 rabbits were killed in a single sheep run. A century and a decade later, Mackenzie Country farmers, still desperate to rid the land of rabbits, took matters into their own hands. They laced baits of oats and carrots with rabbit calicivirus, a haemorrhagic disease that had devastated populations of introduced rabbits in southern Australia. The illegal ploy knocked rabbit numbers into submission, and the New Zealand government subsequently allowed controlled introductions of the virus. However, rabbits have since developed immunity to the virus and their numbers are again rising and endangering the food supply of both sheep and wildlife.[9]
>
> In July, 2009, Environment Canterbury agreed to the Department of Conservation making aerial drops of baits laced with the poisons 1080 and Pindone on 37 000 hectares of the Mackenzie Basin, upper Waitaki Valley, and Aoraki-Mount Cook National Park for the next ten years in an attempt to control rabbit numbers.[10]

As we drive north, steeper hills and grazing beef cattle lead us from Omarama toward Twizel. In the northwest, the snow- and ice-covered crowns of the Ben Ohau Range rear above foothills that look like the wrinkled, spreading paws of giant sphinxes, lined up side by side. As a warning to those who, like us, may be hurrying home, a road sign declares baldly: THE FASTER YOU GO THE BIGGER THE MESS.

North of Twizel, we pause at Mount Cook Lookout on narrow turquoise Lake Pūkākī. Faraway peaks at the lake's northwest end, including those lofty mountains named for the illustrious explorers, James Cook and Abel Tasman, are hidden by cloud. As we travel north toward Lake Tekapō and Two Thumb Range, minor peaks to the west roll stark and open across the landscape. In contrast, eastern peaks brood mysteriously. Clouds cling to their summits and creep down gullies and slopes.

"This big country is unexpected here in New Zealand," Vilis comments, referring to the expansive view. I agree. New Zealand is a small country, and so far in our explorations, we've encountered an array of landscapes rubbing up against each other within a two- or three-hour drive. Mackenzie Country has the feel of a great expanse, such as Canada's prairie.

We marvel at a waterfall of cloud suspended like a hanging glacier above Lake Tekapō. East of Burkes Pass, the landscape exchanges the basin's big country for pastures and rolling, treed hills. We angle northeast to Fairlie and then Geraldine. The hills recede, and we're called homeward by the hedge-bordered fields of the Canterbury Plain.

December 2

AS MY family unpacks from our Queenstown excursion, hydrangeas in our yard open blue parasols of blossoms and roses flame with rich colour and scented beauty in nearly every yard in Lincoln. In between washing loads of dirty clothes, I list homeschooling assignments and writing work to be completed, and house and yard chores to be done to prepare the old clapboard bungalow on North Belt for our upcoming six-week absence. Vilis books us ferry passage from Picton, on South Island's north-eastern tip, to Wellington, the capital city of New Zealand. After completing the booking, he lists field and camping gear we'll need during our stint on North Island, as well as research equipment to be purchased. I wonder what we'll see when we return to South Island. Faded roses in Lincoln's walled yards? Ripened tomatoes in my small garden? The pervasive yellow of late summer?

After we finish unpacking, Vilis heads for Lincoln Medical Centre, concerned about increased redness and swelling around stitches in his left hand, which he accidentally slashed while tinkering with our toaster a week ago. He returns without stitches. Instead, strips of tape hold the wound edges together. "The doctor said it's a sensitivity to the stitches that caused the redness," he says. Once again, my husband elevates his injured hand in a sling.

In mid-morning, Jānis and I drive to the Alpine Ice Sports Centre in Christchurch to skate in a dress rehearsal for the *Cartoon Capers* ice show, which the Centaurus Ice Skating Club will present next weekend. Jānis skated in ice shows in Nova Scotia, but he's nervous about this one far from home. I've never skated in an ice show and have only two and a half months of lessons under my blades. I'm nervous, too.

Upon our arrival at the rink with its mountain-painted walls, I don't envy the half-dozen harried coaches I see attempting to organize seventy or eighty young skaters into their respective groups. I admire their patience as they try to keep the kids quiet, while dealing with props, music, and lights. At the back of the rink, the costume crew is working full out, sorting, assigning, and collecting costumes. The mothers have done a fabulous job of sewing over-one-shoulder, spotted dresses for the *George of the Jungle* number, fuzzy pink elephant costumes for *Dumbo*, zebra costumes plus Simba's entourage of a mongoose, warthog, and hornbill for *The Lion King*, a dozen ghost costumes for *Casper*, an entire undersea community for *The Little Mermaid*, and a complete wardrobe for *Snow White and the Seven Dwarves*, including the evil-minded witch with the poisoned apple.

The rehearsal gets off to a tangled start when *George's* rope catches in a slit between glass panels above the boards, jerking the coach, who is swinging across the ice in the jumping harness, to a more abrupt halt than he anticipated. In the *Scooby-Doo* routine, one of the wee KiwiSkaters who is dressed as a dog is completely disoriented and wanders the ice like a lost puppy looking for its doghouse.

In spite of the glitches, the rehearsal continues from start to finish. Jānis skates in his *Loony Tunes* group number and, with no time to change costumes, frantically squeezes his regular skating clothes into a skin-tight speed-skating suit for his *Speed Racer* group number. Six line-dancers from my Coffee Club adult class perform our routine choreographed to the Chipmunks' version of the country pop song *Achy Breaky Heart*. Sabrina, the skater who's become my buddy, partners me for the opening steps of the routine. Then the six of us move into formation to execute a weave-through, a kickline, and pinwheels. These manoeuvres are the result of hours of practicing together since late October. As nervous as we are, we hear applause from other skaters and coaches when we exit the ice. I release a relieved breath.

IN THE heat of late afternoon, the scent of lemon flowers on the tree beside the bungalow's back door is pungent and pervasive, enticing bees to explore the depths of the purple-edged white blossoms. Before supper, Jānis plucked an orange-yellow lemon to squeeze onto our slow-fried supper of *warehou*, a South Pacific fish. The lemon's mild, full-bodied flavour and colour differ significantly from the sour, bright yellow lemons we're accustomed to buying in Canada.

Jānis tells us that he also saw small green lemons on the tree, and I envision the whole gamut of lemon reproduction occurring at the same time, which sparks a metaphor for life. I say, "Maybe our plans, our goals, should be like that lemon tree."

Vilis looks at me, surprised. "In what way?"

"In that we should have lots of goals in different stages. Some, just buds or ideas. Some beginning to flower. Some, green fruits on their way to being fulfilled. And some, mature, ripened fruits where we can say, 'Hey, we wanted to do this, and we did it!' "

My husband's reply is noncommittal, yet our dream of exploring a faraway country expands and ripens with every day we spend in New Zealand.

December 8

THIS MORNING I belt out lyrics from an old show tune my family sang as members of a community choral group back home in Nova Scotia. The song is lively and jazzy and all about doing a show *right*. I hope it'll alleviate some of Jānis's jitters about skating in the ice show this evening, the first of three back-to-back evening performances this weekend.

Jānis rolls his eyes and tries to suppress a grin, but he can't resist joining in. Dainis does, too.

After the song, our morning passes peacefully, with the boys in separate classrooms: Jānis in the kitchen; Dainis in the living room. Jānis's usual protests over math speed drills and cursive writing appear half-hearted, and he's positively alight with excitement during his spelling lesson. On rare days, the atmosphere in our "school" is totally different. Then, the boys rail against their workbooks, against each other, against me. On those days, homeschooling seems a complete failure, however today, as on the majority of our days, homeschooling is a joy.

IN EARLY evening, icy wind blasts around the corner of the Alpine Ice Sports Centre as Jānis and I collect a Tweety mask and speed skating suit from the costume crew set up outside the rink's back doors. My nine-year-old's face is tight, his eyes shadowed with anxiety.

"What if I don't go on at the right time?" he asks.

"You'll be fine," I say calmly. "Just stick with the other skaters in your numbers and go on when they do."

"But what if I don't have time to change?"

"You will. Right after *Loony Tunes*, take your skates off, pull the speed skating suit on over your skating costume, and put your skates back on."

From the stands, I watch him skate onto the ice with seven other *Loony Tunes* characters costumed to reflect various sports. He's a figure skater. His puffy-sleeved, creamy competition shirt shimmers in the spotlights. The huge yellow Tweety mask that obscures his head bulges bizarrely above his slight body. Right on cue, he performs a split jump, then a shoot-the-duck (a manoeuvre in which he crouches down and extends one leg straight out in front of him), a flip jump, and a few big waltz jumps as the skaters push hard around the rink before exiting the ice. That's one down.

Now it's my turn. Behind the black curtains enclosing a warm-up area at the end of the rink, the ice is shadowed and cluttered with skaters awaiting their numbers. I shiver with nerves and cold as I join nine other women to practice the opening steps for our *Achy Breaky Heart* routine. When the announcer introduces our number, I glide through the gap in the black curtains, my heart pounding. I sense hesitation in the other skaters, too (opening night jitters), but once the music rolls, we step into the routine. Our actual performance passes in a blur, a split second tossed from beginning to end. As we skate back behind the black curtains to exit the ice, we toss each other electric smiles.

In this moment, I realize that the true benefit of participating in the ice show isn't in the performance itself, but in the camaraderie that has accompanied weeks of learning new skills while working together. These women, so open in their welcome to me, so willing to encourage me as I've struggled to learn correct skating technique, have become like sisters. Living in a household with three males, I need this sisterhood. I need the female perspective, the female response to the montage of events and circumstances that make up our lives. Politics and new pants. Kids and the Kiwi dollar. Concern over a husband's accident. Celebrating a wedding anniversary. Letting go of the past and striving to reach new goals. We share these topics in pairs or small clusters, or as in the case of our *Achy Breaky Heart* performance, as a team.

I rush off the ice and hustle around the boards past the curtains to a spot where I can watch Jānis and the other *Speed Racer* performers. Costumed in speed skating suits and cardboard "race cars," they zoom around the rink and jump over low obstacles in their path.

"I could hardly see in that Tweety mask," Jānis tells me after the show, "and I kept worrying that my car would fall down." Yet, excitement and satisfaction lace his voice.

Outside the rink, the wind is even colder than it was earlier. I shiver and cough while driving to Lincoln.

December 9

MY CHEST feels as though it's compressed by a weight, and my breath erupts into hoarse, painful coughing. Exhausted and ill with a chest cold that came on last evening, I wander Lincoln streets with Jānis while Dainis waits to play a tennis match against a Southbridge opponent. Vilis is in Christchurch, purchasing research supplies: topographical maps, corrugated plastic tree protectors to be used as tracking tunnels, paraffin oil and powdered charcoal to create track-collecting medium, neon orange flagging tape to mark trap and tracking tunnel locations, synthetic fibre batting for stoat bedding in traps, and plastic storage tubs for field gear. The time is near. We leave for North Island in five days.

This morning, the commercial section of Lincoln's main drag, Gerald Street, is closed to traffic in honour of the annual Lincoln Pageant Day. Sidewalk vendors sell roses and other perennial flowers, bedding plants, Christmas baking, needlework crafts, pottery, preserves, and raffle tickets. While browsing, Jānis and I meet "Raksha," a Cub leader. She asks if Jānis plans to join the other Cubs on the float in the parade. He and I exchange startled looks and rush home to gather his Cub uniform. Then we jog to the Ellesmere Country Club where the floats are being assembled.

With Jānis delivered to his Cub leaders, I hurry to the tennis courts to watch Dainis in action. I arrive in time to catch the end of his first set, which he wins. While he waits for his next set, I'm lured back to Gerald Street by the sound of pipers, arriving just in time for the Pageant Day parade.

The procession is small, but full of smiles and waves, with a rugby float, two plump ponies, a pre-school float, a couple of donkeys, a pair of clowns, Donald Duck riding a bicycle, a float of Lincoln parishes, and what seems a discordant juxtaposition of Scottish pipers and a van advertising a pop music station. A tractor pulls the Cub/Scout float that Dainis and other Scouts decorated last evening. They wrapped a trailer box with black plastic they'd painted with Christmas trees, stars, and a sleigh pulled by a lone reindeer, and then decorated the trailer with balloons and streamers. When the float passes, I grin and wave at "Akela" Andrew Wallace and Raksha and the half-dozen waving Cubs, including Jānis. In his tan Canadian Cub shirt and navy beret he stands out among the Lincoln Cubs who are clad in dark-green jumpers (pullover sweaters). I laugh when the children toss handfuls of candy in my direction, and reach to the pavement to retrieve the sweets.

Once the parade passes, I rush back to the tennis courts, feeling like a yo-yo flung out by one child and reeled back by the other. "The parade's coming down North Belt now," I tell Dainis, showing him my stash of candy.

His eyes widen. "I'm going to watch the parade!" he tells Nancy Borrie, who's in charge of the competition. Nancy has a heart for young people and has been a tremendous encouragement to Dainis during his tennis lessons. She instantly calls a temporary halt to play, and the young athletes sprint for the street, laughter trailing in their wake.

I jog to the country club to collect Jānis after the parade, then we return to the courts to watch Dainis play his next set. During the afternoon, I rest, storing up energy for another ice show marathon of waiting followed by a brief spot in the light.

December 10

THE BLACK Cat ferry lies sleek and powerful at the dock in Lyttelton, awaiting its departure to Quail Island. The harbour town bustles with dockyard noise, and graceful yachts rest in the marina. Lyttelton, which is Christchurch's link to the world's commerce, nestles on the shore of turquoise Lyttelton Harbour, the drowned crater of extinct Lyttelton Volcano. This volcano and equally extinct Akaroa Volcano comprise Banks Peninsula, a bud of land that juts thirty kilometres

LYTTELTON HARBOUR AND QUAIL ISLAND

into the Pacific Ocean southeast of Christchurch. The peninsula, with its tawny hills and spectacular views spanning half the breadth of South Island, is a quick drive from Lincoln and has become my family's hiking "backyard." Today, I see little sign of the damage inflicted by mid-October's hurricane-force winds that sank a dozen yachts and tore jetties apart.

Along with other Cub and Scout families, Vilis, the boys, and I board the ferry to attend a year-end picnic on the island we've seen so often during our explorations of Crater Rim Walkway and Summit Road in the Port Hills. Named in 1842, for a now-extinct New Zealand quail, the island lies near the centre of Lyttelton Harbour and is an erosion-resistant basalt remnant of the crater floor. In the Māori language, the island is called Ōtamahua, meaning "The Place where Children Gathered Sea Birds' Eggs."[11]

We ride the ferry for ten minutes, then disembark at a jetty on Quail Island's eastern tip. Our group gathers in the shade of trees, and Mike Bowie, an entomologist at Lincoln University and father of a Cub and Scout, informs us that volunteers are working to increase the island's biodiversity by restoring populations of native plants, birds, reptiles, and insects. "This island was named for a bird that's now extinct," Mike tells us. "Does anyone know the Māori name for that bird?"

Jānis's hand shoots up. "*Koreke.*"

Mike nods. "That's right."

As Mike continues with his presentation, Vilis whispers to Jānis. "How did you know that?"

Our son shrugs self-consciously. "Our Cub pack is named after it."

Mike informs us that an ecological restoration trust is in the process of planting trees and aims to return a third of the island's eighty-five hectares (most of which are now covered by grassland) to native coastal forest. The trust's volunteers are also ridding the island of weeds and pest animals with the hope that it can become a sanctuary for local native plant and animal species that are rare or threatened on the mainland. He slides back the lid of a long, slim wooden box he's holding and shows us a tree *wētā*. It's a large, wingless, grasshopperlike insect that's rare on Banks Peninsula due to habitat destruction. This species will be returned to Quail Island in an attempt to preserve it in the wild. I'm impressed with the trust's vision and its volunteers' dedication.

After Mike's presentation, everyone tackles a hiking track that follows the island's perimeter. It leads us past a single white wooden cross in a small graveyard surrounded by a white picket fence. The fence guards the remains of Ivor Skelton (1898-1923), a member of a leper colony quarantined on the island in 1907. Also quarantined on the island were nineteenth-century immigrants who arrived after long sea voyages, livestock imported from England, and the sled dogs, ponies, and mules of Antarctic explorers Robert Falcon Scott and Ernest Shackleton. All this I learn by reading an information leaflet provided by the Black Cat Group.

At the island's western tip, the remains of boats and small ships rise from the beach and shallow water like fossilized ribs of mosasaurs. A boy magnet, the ship graveyard lures Cubs and Scouts into a downhill race to the shore to inspect the derelicts. One is a small steamship with a rusty boiler, another is a wooden ship bolted and banded with iron, and a third is a broad boat with a tin-covered wooden hull and iron ribs. Scattered pieces of wood and metal indicate other watercraft. A plaque states that the first boat to run aground in the Quail Island shallows was the *Novelty*, a small paddle steamer that met its demise in 1887. The plaque also lists eight other vessels whose bones litter this shore.

QUAIL ISLAND SHIP GRAVEYARD

The Cubs and Scouts race from one wreck's remains to another. Some, like Dainis, climb partway up the hull of the iron-banded wooden ship. Several, including Jānis, scramble up onto the rusty boiler, with grey-haired Akela Andrew Wallace in their midst. Andrew is a fabulous Cub leader and has gone out of his way to welcome Jānis since my son's first Cub meeting in mid-August.

Eventually, Andrew urges the boys to return to the track, and we tramp through grasslands above steep cliffs on the island's northern perimeter. After crossing a neck of land, we picnic in shade near a jetty. The Cubs and Scouts squeeze in a short game of beach cricket before the Black Cat ferry arrives to purr us back across the harbour to Lyttelton.

PERHAPS IT takes two performances to work out all the kinks. Tonight is the best performance yet for Jānis's *Loony Tunes* group in the ice show (the *Speed Racer* number went better last night), and it's my group's best performance, too. When I skate out for the Grand Finale, I truly feel like I'm a part of this production, and when the *Achy Breaky Heart* team hams it up for photographs after the show, I'm giddy with the celebration that accompanies final-night success. Vilis, who along with Dainis attended the show tonight, snaps pictures of me with the other skaters. As we leave the rink, he wraps an arm around me and gives me a congratulatory squeeze.

December 13

IN THE heat of a summer's eve, after tent seams are sealed, weeds are jerked from the gardens, and backpacks are filled with clothes to last six weeks away from North Belt, my husband, sons, and I slam tennis balls at one another on the Lincoln courts. This afternoon, Dainis placed second in the Lincoln club tournament. His hits are calculated and confident. Jānis's are pure power unleashed. Vilis's are decorated with spins and angles. Mine are inexperienced attempts to simply return the volley.

The hot air around us is a complete contrast to yesterday morning, when mist hung above the rink ice and breathed condensation onto the glass panels, its damp cold a refreshing contrast to the heat outdoors. I skated on and on during my hour-long Coffee Club lesson, stretching my glides, my mind wanting to do so much more than my body has learned. In the midst of an instrumental rendition of *Silent Night* I realized that my fingers were cold and I could see my breath. For the first time in this country, the feeling was right for Christmas.

Vilis and the boys joined me for Coffee Club's lively Christmas party in the warm room, Zamboni's, after skating. Daphne wore red velvet reindeer antlers on her frizzy red hair. Sabrina played her guitar while she and Daphne led skating revellers in singing Christmas carols. I mentioned to some that I'd be away for six weeks and received wishes of 'Merry Christmas! See you when you get back.' When my family exited the rink, hot air swallowed us. The boys ran to a pile of melting snow dumped by the Zamboni and grabbed handfuls, firing snowballs at Vilis and me as we ducked behind our station wagon's hot blue body.

December 14

BEFORE DEPARTING Lincoln, I take a last look at our secluded North Belt yard. The two shrub fuchsias are glorious. They drip blossoms among green lanceolate leaves on woody twigs. One shrub's blossoms are such a pale shade of pink they're almost white with rosy hearts. The other's are far less chaste, capturing the eye with sultry hot pink skirts and violet centres.

It's 11:00 a.m. and hot, the sky a woven tapestry of white ruffles and grey streaks on blue warp as Vilis, the boys, and I pile into the Blue Bomb. Our destination is the stoat research site in Tongariro Forest Conservation Area, 330 kilometres north of Wellington, and 770 kilometres north of Lincoln. We'll take three days to make the trip, pausing to hike at Kaikōura, a coastal town about two-thirds of the way between Lincoln and the ferry terminal in Picton.

As we drive north from Lincoln, I note that summer heat has tinged pastures brown and yellow on the Canterbury Plain, yet crops of barley and canola stand tall and green. North of Christchurch, yellow-flowering shrub lupins edge the highway, and I spot another sign with a message for drivers. This one states:

DRINK

DrIvE

A patchwork of pine plantations and pastures covers the hills around Waipara. Another poster sign displays a photograph of a speedometer with a white cross rather than a speedometer needle resting on the 140-kilometre-per-hour mark. Yesterday, Radio New Zealand National reported a crack-down on speeders. Now, anyone exceeding the limit of 100 kilometres per hour by more than 10 kilometres per hour will be ticketed. The police, whose presence on the highways seems to be practically nonexistent, rely on speed cameras placed at intervals along highways to catch speeders.

So far, the route is familiar. We drove it in mid-September, except then we turned northwest, heading for Lewis Pass and beyond that, Tūtaki Valley in the Buller District of northwestern South Island. There, Vilis helped three Landcare Research technicians dismantle radio-telemetry towers used in a former brushtail possum removal study while the boys and I hiked and birded in misty pastures and forests.

Today, we continue northward, the highway leading us into new territory. "It looks like the Canterbury Plain has gotten narrower," Vilis comments.

To the west, foothills of the Puketeraki Range push upward, cutting into the level plain. To the east, rounded, lumpy hills jut into the sky. On the plain, irrigation pipes spray water onto fields. Black-and-white magpies scavenge roadkill, and Australasian harriers (slim brown open-country hawks) cruise the sky on V-wings. Huge, round hay bales in a field look like toys left by a giant who was distracted from an orderly game.

The Bomb, sluggish with four bicycles atop her plus four passengers and six weeks' worth of research and personal gear inside her, labours uphill when we enter the Lowry Peaks Range. Here, pastoral hills support vineyards and paddocks that hold sheep, dairy cattle, beef cattle, and red deer.

"They look wilder when they stand in that long grass," Vilis murmurs, referring to the deer. Perhaps he's reminded of the white-tailed deer in our unkempt meadows in Nova Scotia, with long grass around their legs and their heads forever lifting, their ears forever cupping the air to detect the sound of approaching danger. These farmed deer have no predators other than the butcher. Such is not the case for the remaining feral deer in this country. As pests, they can be hunted year-round; thus, they avoid humanity. "You never see them down here," Landcare technician Morgan Coleman told us as we neared Lincoln after the Tūtaki Valley trip. "They stay back in the hills where they have some cover."

North of Hurunui River, a narrow plain gives way to rolling hills, beyond which we descend onto another narrow plain at Cheviot. Hundreds of European starlings flush into the air from cut, drying hay. A low-flying harrier almost collides with the car's windshield. The plain lifts into small, pointed hills, and the road curves tightly to follow their undulations.

"The hills are shrubbier now," Vilis notes.

"A lot of it's broom," I tell him. Scotch broom was introduced to New Zealand by English settlers more than a century ago and is now classified as a noxious invasive weed of pastures, forestry sites, and native ecosystems.[12]

"So they've lost out on everything," my husband comments, referring to local pastoralists (sheep and cattle farmers). "They no longer have native bush and can't graze livestock either."

Farther north, large thickets of low-crowned, shrubby *mānuka* cloak the hillsides, the native trees' silvery-white blossoms resembling a shiny glaze in the glare of the afternoon sun. The highway dips and climbs and curves, the speed limit often dropping to 35 kilometres per hour. When we begin our descent out of the hills, Vilis and I spot a tongue of land jutting into hazy blue water.

I announce, "Dainis, Jānis, look! It's the Kaikōura Peninsula."

The boys' heads jerk up out of the books in which they've been immersed since we left Lincoln.

"That's where we're going tramping and maybe whale watching," I tell them.

"Neat." Dainis ducks into his book again.

"How much of that is actually the Kaikōura Peninsula?" Jānis asks.

"All of it." I regale him with information gleaned from a guidebook. "It's an area surrounded by ocean extremely rich in marine life. There's a sharp drop-off in the land off the coast, resulting in very deep cold water not far from shore. So it's a place where the deep cold water, with all its nutrients and plankton and krill, mixes with shallower warm water. That creates a great feeding ground for all kinds of marine animals, including sperm whales all year long, humpback whales in winter, and orcas in summer. Plus dolphins."[13]

The air wafting through the car's open windows is noticeably cooler.

"Ah, ocean air." Vilis smiles at me, and we declare a temporary book ban, instructing the boys to read the scenery instead. To our left, steep forested mountainsides plunge to the highway. To our right, blue-green surf smashes against offshore rocks and throws salty white froth to the sky.

Kaikōura is a small town on the peninsula's north shore. It lists tourism as its first industry, and the town centre is devoted to various marine tours: whale-watching, swimming with dolphins, kayaking with fur seals. We spot our first live hedgehog trundling to hide beneath the visitor centre's porch. Its head is unexpectedly large, its prickly body an oval of spines above tiny feet.

Inside the visitor centre, we read listings for various outings and gulp at the prices of some, including whale watching which costs ninety-five dollars per person. In the end, we decide to tramp the eleven-kilometre Peninsula Walkway tomorrow. A full-day outing that features breeding colonies of southern fur seals and gulls, it'll cost us nothing but stamina.

A campground beside Lyell Creek offers us shelter for the night within easy walking distance of the town centre. Trees shade our tent site, and the songs of goldfinches, fantails, and grey warblers light the air with bright music.

While Dainis positions our tent to give us a little privacy, Jānis chops onions for hamburgers and then slices cucumbers and tomatoes. After their chores. the boys bounce and leap on the campground trampoline until our evening meal or "tea" is ready.

After tea, we stroll the Kaikōura shore, its pebbles a grey gown decorated with streamers of green, burgundy, yellow, and brown kelps and other seaweeds. Ocean mist thickens the air, and surf pounds onto the beach, churning stones and seaweed within frothing curves and lace. To the west, the imposing mountains of the Seaward Kaikōura Range brood above a blanket of fog. Like a blurred photograph, they reveal image upon image of overlapping peak and jutting headland.

Vilis and the boys play a wave-racing game, trying to stay just out of reach of the incoming rush of water. Some waves form gentle arcs and are easily evaded. Others build into huge walls of water that smash onto shore, leap up the pebbled incline, and spit salt water as they grab at racing feet.

Vilis leaves the game and joins me higher on the shore. "This is what you do when you need to sort your life out," he muses. "Walk on a beach like this."

"*Mmm*. Looking onward..." I nod to the veiled mountains, "Onward to where some things are barely glimpsed, others still hidden and unseen, as in life." *And where each day is a step toward that distant, veiled future.* I think back to the months before Vilis received confirmation of funding for the stoat research that brought us to New Zealand. Caught up in the responsibilities of motherhood, homeschooling, driving my sons to their many activities, caring for our property, and growing food, I yearned for an escape, for an adventure far from home and all my commitments.

And now we're here, half-way around the world from our home, gazing at brooding New Zealand mountains and dodging South Pacific waves. Dreams really do come true.

Even after Dainis abandons the wave-racing game, Jānis continues to pit himself against nature. On the pebbly shore, he stretches down to grab up handfuls of wave froth, as if to say, "I got you!" At least three times he's caught by the ocean's fingers, and once the surf rolled up past his ankles. Finally, he joins the rest of us high on the beach. We find wave-tossed shells of snails and *pāua* (abalone), a dead fish, a crab, a sea star (starfish), and clusters of round orange, yellow, and white air bladders of an unknown ocean algae. I call the last "beach grapes," and the boys pop the bladders' sun-dried skins with delight.

The beach lures us onward, its western expanse unbroken by human figures. Two black-phase oystercatchers – large black shorebirds with long red bills – allow us to cross their patch of pebbles. Farther along the shore, we approach an intriguing ensemble of items in a casual cluster: a tattered car seat and the bottom half of another car seat, a torn easy chair, a huge driftwood log, a rusted iron stove, and a woven metal fire basket shaped like a barrel. Vilis sinks into the easy chair with a sigh. I sit on the driftwood log beside him. The boys scurry about, gathering tinder and dry wood to construct small fires.

KAIKŌURA COAST

At 6:25 p.m., the light is as dim and brooding as if it were three hours later. I look at the mountains of the Seaward Kaikōura Range, with snow covering the highest peaks, and envision only wilderness beyond them. It's as though I'm once again at Alexandra Fiord in Canada's High Arctic, where I researched plant communities at a polar "oasis" in the early eighties. There, I looked out across the moodily lit fiord to Thorvald Peninsula and the rest of Ellesmere Island beyond. No surf pounded; rather, ice floes and minor bergs lay stranded on the shore. The Arctic Ocean was never this clear green; instead, always a cold royal blue. Yet, I felt the same power of ocean, of rock, of air thick with wildness.

I glance behind me and am disappointed to see other people on the beach. Beyond them lies the town of Kaikōura and beyond that, the peninsula we'll tramp around and over tomorrow. It's a plateau scarred by rugged, vertical cliffs.

The driftwood log I'm sitting on vibrates as a train passes by on a track inshore from the pebble beach. Vilis closes his eyes. The boys build small heaps of gathered twigs, and Jānis is successful coaxing his into flames. At Dainis's suggestion, they consolidate their two piles of twigs into one, and I think that my older son, with his gentle and logical persuasion, may one day become a diplomat. I slide onto the ground and lie beside the log, closing my eyes. Rounded beach pebbles nudge my back, and the fire's warmth touches my legs while the pungent, familiar scent of wood smoke fills the air.

December 15

LAST EVENING, we encountered rusted fire implements on the pebbled shore west of Kaikōura. This morning, we come across a brick and cement chimney on the shore above the high tide mark at Kaikōura's east end. The chimney is all that remains of the Customs House in what was the port of Kaikōura before it was moved west to its present site in 1909.

KAIKŌURA'S HISTORY
In 1842 Robert Fyffe established the Waipuka shore whaling station here, the first European settlement on Kaikōura Peninsula. He also built Fyffe House, which has been restored and painted bright pink and stands near the Customs House chimney. By 1869, the whaling station had blossomed into the port of Kaikōura, which maintained its importance as a shipping and commercial centre until the time of the port's relocation. Hundreds of years before Mr. Fyffe appeared on the scene, Māori fished, hunted birds, and gardened in the Kaikōura area. All this we learn from an interpretive display co-sponsored by The Community Trust, Department of Conservation, and New Zealand Historic Places Trust.

DAINIS AND CUSTOMS HOUSE CHIMNEY, KAIKŌURA

It seems an odd place for a port. Limestone cliffs rear up at our backs, and rippled, stacked layers of limestone, coarse and rough like torn corrugated cardboard, protrude from white-laced water offshore. Yet, the lure of whales was here then, as it is now.

Dainis finds a streamer of storm-washed kelp on high ground behind the interpretive sign. Its stipe is a thick tube and its blade a long, flat oval that reminds me of a beaver's tail, although much longer. "It feels like leather," he says, pressing the blade.

"It feels like foam," Vilis contradicts.

"Let's see what it's like inside." Dainis cuts into the kelp with his pocket knife.

"It *is* foam!" we all exclaim, amazed at the closely packed air bubbles formed by spongy yellow tissues within the blade. Thus begins our exploration of Peninsula Walkway.

The cliffs behind us give way to sheep pastures terraced by countless hooves. The offshore rocks are replaced by a sandy beach. Two young cyclists ride to the edge of a pool and point at a dead eel floating among brown weeds.

Farther along on our hike, a sheet of grey rock replaces the beach, creating a stark, monotonic landscape that stretches thirty metres to the breaking surf. Its seaward edge is broken by a stalking white-faced heron, a pied shag (cormorant) perched like a black-and-white sentinel on the rock lip, and two brown-flecked turnstones flipping exposed seaweeds with their beaks. My interest in birds leads me to wonder where home is for the turnstones. Is it their arctic breeding grounds, where the sun shines endlessly during brief summers, or the Southern Hemisphere, where food and warmth are readily available while the Northern Hemisphere is locked in winter?

We watch our feet as we walk, avoiding shallow pools of water that sheet the grey rock, wetting snails and bladder wrack. I dawdle, observing the birds. Vilis and the boys are twenty metres ahead of me when a huge rusty-brown shape rears up and roars at Vilis. Startled almost out of his skin, he leaps back amid laughter from two men standing in a parking area at the end of the road that parallels the shore. The rusty-brown shape, which is a southern fur seal, slumps into rest, having cleared its personal space of intruders.

"We thought you saw him," one of the bystanders calls out.

"Well, I know he's there now," Vilis replies, his voice shaking.

We've arrived quite memorably at the Point Kean fur seal colony. As we scramble from the seal's rocky realm to the car park, the marine mammal squirms restlessly, then roars at one of the two men who had gotten too close. The seal gives up its resting location and drags itself away, its shoulders hunched into pointed mountains.

A sheep bleats on the hillside behind us, an odd juxtaposition of sound to the seal's roar. On one side of us is the natural world at land's edge, slipping into the ocean that humans have not yet tamed.

To the other side is the manipulated terrestrial landscape dominated by humans and their domestic beasts. I wonder what this spot looked like when Robert Fyffe first sailed this way. Did any native forests still grow on the hills and plateau, or had the Māori already burned them to create gardens?

Offshore, an Australasian gannet – large white seabird with black wing edges and a yellow-washed head – dives from the sky into the ocean, fishing in spectacular style before flapping its wings to lift into the air. An interpretive display informs us that fur seals also dive for food and may stay under water for thirty minutes and dive to 200 metres in search of octopus, squid, lantern fish, and other prey.

"How can seals stay under water for thirty minutes when the best human divers without oxygen can only stay under for *five* minutes?" Dainis asks.

"Do you remember how that works, Magi?" Vilis tosses me the question.

I perk up. I *love* talking to my kids about biology. "It's a physiological response. If I remember correctly, it's called the diving response. The seal's heart rate drops really low, and it uses far less oxygen than normal. That allows it to stay down a long time. Diving ducks do the same thing."

We walk across the car park and descend stone steps onto the rocky shore.

"Here's another of those kelps with the foamy holdfasts," Jānis calls out, holding up the same type of broad-bladed kelp we examined earlier.

"That part is the blade," I tell him. "The holdfast is just this bottom part." I show him grasping finger-like projections at the end of the kelp opposite to the blade. "It keeps the kelp attached to the ocean bottom or to rocks." Now I point to the thick, tubular stalk.

"This is called the stipe." I touch the blade. "All that foamy tissue is for buoyancy, to keep the kelp blade up in the water so it can get light."

"It's big," Jānis comments.

"It is." The entire kelp stretches a metre and a half, dwarfing the smaller wracks (brown seashore algae) we've seen on this rocky shore. "Some kelps grow to be hundreds of feet long," I tell my sons. "They're like forests under the ocean and provide a place for all kinds of marine animals to live."

Dainis nods. "I've read about that."

"Of course, the kelps aren't the same kinds of plants as trees," I add. "They're algae."

"This is an *algae?*" Jānis holds up the kelp.

"Yes."

As we tramp on, I think that this is what homeschooling is all about. In the past five minutes, we've touched on vertebrate physiology, plant taxonomy, and marine ecology in one curious sweep using very real, very immediate examples.

At our feet, brown algae with beaded air bladders that look like pearl necklaces inhabit tide pools, as do snails and their conical-shelled cousins, limpets. Outside the tide pools, more snails and limpets cling to rocks, unmoving. I glance up at the sun and tell Dainis, "The intertidal zone, the part of the shore exposed between high and low tides, is a harsh place to live when the tide's out. It's hot and dry. These snails are just hanging in there until the tide comes back in."

The snails are everywhere. Tiny black-shelled ones and medium-sized, grey-shelled ones. It's hard to avoid stepping on them. Dainis kicks a large one loose from the rock surface. "Oops! What will happen to this one now?" he asks, picking up the dislodged snail.

"It'll be all right," I tell him. "See, it's closing its operculum, its little door. That will help it maintain some moisture until the tide returns."

"Let's put it in a tide pool and see what happens!" He skips over to the nearest tide pool and releases the snail beneath the water surface. Almost immediately, we see a dark grey body appear beneath the shell, its eyes raised high on stalks above its head. Dainis grins and, dodging snails, skips on to catch up with Vilis and Jānis.

I putter along behind, my attention caught by a little shag diving for food among kelp blades that swirl and roll in the rough water. Again and again, the sleek black-bodied bird dives beneath the water. It emerges with a slender fish and gulps it down.

Halfway around the track, we pause to picnic on a white pebble beach. The boys build a tiny fire with dry flax bits and driftwood twigs, and we roast strawberry and vanilla marshmallows over the flames. When we finish, my sons laugh while carrying seawater in leaky plastic bags to douse the fire. The shore beside us is draped with satiny sea lettuce, the green algae providing a vivid backdrop for beaded necklaces of bladder wrack jumbled onto it by the receding tide.

Ahead, people are visible on folded rocks offshore. And so are seals: seals scratching lazily, seals climbing out of the water, seals sleeping, seals with fluid bodies pouring over rocks. The marine mammals appear unconcerned by the presence of humans as long as their personal space isn't invaded. This makes it easy to understand how their populations were decimated by club-wielding and gun-toting sealers in the late eighteenth century. We jump from one craggy, serrated rock to another and join the seal-watchers. On our arrival, a big seal lazily lifts a flipper to scratch itself, before shifting its body to a more comfortable sleeping position.

"That's what I did last night," I say, laughing, in reference to my nocturnal tossing and turning while trying to find a soft spot on the tent floor, "but that seal has a lot more padding than I do!"

Vilis gestures to the scene before us. "We don't need to kayak among the seals. We can walk among them right here."

It's true. We're in the middle of the breeding colony. We spot sleek dark-brown bodies tucked into nooks and crannies in every direction and more seals on rocks farther offshore. While exploring, we're startled again and again by seals lifting their heads, alerting us to their presence in cracks or under ledges a few metres away.

BLACK-BACKED GULLS AND SOUTHERN FUR SEAL AT POINT KEAN

Red-billed and black-backed gulls also breed on the serrated rocks, their shrill squawks filling the air. The gulls incubate eggs, stand protectively near nests, flutter about the rocks, and hover in the air. We almost step on a nest containing two large olive-green eggs with black splotches in an untidy cup constructed of plucked grasses and gathered twigs. Shell pieces from a recently broken egg lie beside the two intact eggs. Which gull species laid the eggs? Is the other species the predator? I see a large black-backed gull standing silent and still near a smaller red-billed gull on its nest. Is the black-back waiting for the red-bill to leave in order to dine on its eggs or chicks? I know gulls are proven nest robbers.

"I like this place," Vilis states, nodding as if to give approval to the seals and gulls. "It's so full of life."

NESTING RED-BILLED GULL, PENINSULA WALKWAY

By now, it's mid-afternoon, and the heat induces us to leave the noisy gulls and sleepy seals. We jump from rock to rock, pausing at tide pools to look into their depths for anemones and for octopuses which Jānis desperately wants to see. We don't find octopuses, but do find shiny black anemones. Some resemble plump, pursed mouths sucked in on themselves on rocks above water level. In a tide pool, others spread short tentacles into circular predatory crowns.

"What's this?" Jānis calls, pointing to a mollusc with an oval, gently rounded shell composed of distinct plates.

"It's a chiton," I tell him. "Do you see how its shell is made up of plates?"

He bends to count them. "Seven."

"Eight, I think."

We roam over the rocks, going wherever our interest takes us. More bits and pieces of long-ago-acquired knowledge resurface in my brain, pulled up by the currents of my sons' curiosity and tossed like flotsam into the open sea of their minds. More than two decades ago, I spent two glorious weeks on a University of Alberta marine biology fieldtrip based on the west coast of Vancouver Island, British Columbia, and northern Washington. Those were two weeks of total immersion in coastal ecosystems, two weeks of experiencing intertidal life with the sole purpose of learning. Some of that learning soaked into my soul. Now, like a gift from my past, it re-emerges as I teach my sons.

When we return to the shoreline path, broken chunks of white limestone roll beneath our feet, making walking difficult. We rest in a pocket of shade created by a limestone cliff and observe red-billed gulls raising elegant beaks to the sky as they swallow fresh water from a small puddle caught in the rocks.

Alerted by a shifting curtain of loud, angry sound, we notice a milling frenzy of red-billed gulls on a rocky point across an inlet. A man wearing a red hard hat and ear protectors moves slowly among them. Through binoculars, I can see his dark blue coat and pants, stained with gull droppings. He's carrying a long-handled net. He stops, stands still, slowly reaches forward, and then scoops a gull from its nest into the net, before deftly removing the bird from the net to hold it in his hands. I provide a play-by-play commentary before lending Vilis and the boys my binoculars.

"He must be banding," Vilis comments. "The sound must be deafening over there."

"Let's go see!" the boys pipe up.

We leave the shade and skirt the inlet. At the edge of the gull colony, birds scream above our heads – the sound level, uncomfortable.

"*Oooh!* Look at all the droppings on him!" Jānis laughs, referring to the biologist, who has his back turned to us. "I wouldn't want to do that."

"Look!" Dainis shouts. "There's another biologist, and he's wearing *shorts*."

He is indeed, and has as many gull droppings on him, and as many gulls screaming at his crouched body as does the other bander.

Vilis grimaces. "Let's get out of here. It's too noisy."

Away from the gulls, we sidle around tall, smooth limestone "flower pots" to avoid more fur seals. Vilis, Dainis, and I creep along a thin, narrow ledge under which one seal lies. "It's a good thing seals don't eat people," I murmur.

"Yeah. They're not grizzlies." Vilis calls quietly to our younger son, who's walking behind the rest of us on rocks closer to the water, "Jānis, watch out for the seal." He points down. As Jānis starts to make a wide circle around the seal, it swings its body around and stares at him.

"Not that way!" I call out hurriedly. "Remember, the sign said not to go between seals and the ocean. Come this way."

Jānis retreats then follows our path along the narrow ledge. Once again, we're on seal alert, and it's a good thing, because we find more in unexpected places as we cautiously make our way along passages between the limestone formations. The marine mammals are inconspicuously everywhere: on ledges above us, in cracks between rocks, in a narrow passageway between a rock tower and cliff. To avoid this last seal, we scramble up and over a limestone outcrop, encountering a dead seal rotting in a shallow pool of water, the air around it fetid.

"*Yuck!* That's what makes the stench." Jānis grimaces and turns away to climb onto a rock outcrop, as does Dainis.

I call them back. "Did you see the seal's large canine teeth? Seals are in the same order of mammals as cats and dogs and other terrestrial carnivores, the Carnivora."

"That's right," Vilis adds. "Even though it lives in the ocean, a seal is more similar to a coyote than a coyote is to a mouse."

"*What?*" Jānis exclaims, then he thinks for a moment. "Oh, yeah. A mouse is a rodent."

We scramble along the rough-pebbled shore littered with driftwood. We're all tired, both from the sun and from the uneven footing we've been walking on, kilometre after kilometre. Yet, when I glance back over my shoulder and see the jagged black edges of a cave beckoning from the shoreline cliff I call out, "There's a sea cave behind us. Do you want to explore it?"

"A sea cave?" Jānis's head jerks up. "You bet!"

At last my younger son has a cave, something he's been wanting to explore ever since our arrival in New Zealand. This one is a high split in dark rock that widens at its base. Its sharp-edged lips enclose us in a dim space that drops gently to a small, lower opening to the shore. We climb down to the lower opening, then up again, the sheer, angled walls beside us showing marked horizontal layers.

"So, what do you think, Jāni?" I ask.

"Good, but not long enough."

As we leave the cave entrance, Dainis stumbles and falls forward down the slope, crying out and landing heavily on his right hip. Thankfully the slope is soft soil, not the "torn-cardboard" jagged rocks we traversed earlier to get close to seals. We rest until Dainis's pain dulls, taking the time to observe a few red-billed gulls nesting on nearby boulders.

"This is a great place, isn't it?" I say quietly to Dainis. "It's different from any of our other hikes. There are things jumping out and yelling at you everywhere."

"Yeah." When he feels ready, we hike on, sticking to higher ground and the rough pebble-and-driftwood shore.

When we round the last point on the peninsula, silence envelopes us. No seals. No gulls. No surf. We hike the edge of a great slab of knobby rock that looks like a giant hand made it by pressing together lumps of modeling clay.

Finally, we reach South Bay, a small community on the opposite side of the peninsula from Kaikōura. Vilis locates the trail leading up over the plateau. It leads us through ungrazed pastures then passes between the overgrown embankments of the Ngāi Niho *pā* (a Māori fortress) atop the plateau. A stone seat positioned to look out over sea and sky welcomes us. A plaque behind the seat states:

> HO HOU TE RONGO
> (UNITE IN PEACE)
> OH! MAORI AND PAKEHA,
> MEDITATE HERE ON UMAN
> GOODWILL, JUSTICE, RACIAL
> UNDERSTANDING, & THE
> STRIVING FOR FRIENDLY
> COOPERATION. IF ATTAINED

THESE COULD BRING PEACE
TO THE WORLD FAMILY

Weary and hungry, we hurry down the hill into Kaikōura, where a hearty supper of fish and chips revives us. Then we walk westward on the brooding pebble beach. The boys light a small fire at the eclectic cluster of beach furniture, but within minutes, rain sweeps inshore. Thunder and lightning send us racing for our tent.

December 16

STEADY RAIN falls while we drive north from Kaikōura toward Blenheim, where we hope to get Dainis's glasses' repaired. The frames lost a wing when the boys collided on the campground trampoline yesterday. Beside us, the Seaward Kaikōura Range plunges to the ocean, cramming railway and highway into a narrow strip between the mountains' rock walls and the ocean's surf. Signs advertise crayfish, which are plentiful in the nutrient-rich waters. Their abundance inspired the peninsula's name, "*kai*" meaning food, and "*kōura*" meaning crayfish.[14]

I mull over the contrast between Queenstown and Kaikōura, both popular South Island tourist destinations, and say to Vilis, "The attraction of Kaikōura for tourists is different from that of Queenstown. It's not as hectic here as Queenstown. In Kaikōura, people come to see living things. In Queenstown, people come to do daredevil, thrill-seeking things. The feel is totally different."

"Yeah, it is," he agrees, "but I can see doing both."

A half hour later, we pull over at the look-off above the Ohau Point seal colony and see hundreds of seals on rocks below us. They bark and roar, their musky odour pervading the air. A small seal nips at a massive bull. Three seals play in a large pool, frolicking and turning summersaults. Offshore, two seals swim in tandem, leaping into the air in graceful arcs. "I didn't know they could jump!" Jānis exclaims. Yesterday, we observed seals at rest, slow and awkward on land. Today, we're given a glimpse of their incredible speed and agility in water.

Beyond Ohau Point, a narrow plain extends between the coast and high hills. Here, the landscape is drier and more sparsely vegetated than near Kaikōura. Fifty kilometres from Blenheim the road turns inland, winding among rolling hills. Sheep are darker in colour than those we've generally seen on South Island, their thick wool grey rather than white. Perhaps it's simply a matter of unsheared versus sheared. Apparently so. Later, we see skinny, sheared sheep that are definitely white. North of Ward, we encounter dry brown hills reminiscent of Otago ranching country. "I thought it would be lush forest," I say, surprised.

LANDSCAPE SOUTH OF BLENHEIM

In Blenheim, we're given directions to a jeweller's shop for the glasses repairs. At noon, with heat pouring in through the Bomb's windows, we drive out of town. A half hour later, Vilis parks the station wagon in a line-up at the Picton ferry terminal, and at 1:30 p.m. the *Arahura* ferries us into Picton Harbour. The surrounding landscape of forested headlands and islands reminds me of Canada's

West Coast. At land's end, a few islands edged with sheer cliffs remain as we leave the sheltered waters for Cook Strait, notorious for the winds and storms that prevented both Abel Tasman and James Cook from sailing into what is now Wellington Harbour.[15]

"I hope we get a storm," Jānis wishes fervently.

Instead, bright sunshine bathes our passage, and the strait's waters never become rougher than what the ferry captain describes as "gentle swells." Jānis spots a seal lounging on its back. It lifts a flipper as though to wave at us. Then he and I identify a squadron of fairy prions – small grey seabirds with pale heads and blue bills. Each bird has a dark *M* across the upper surface of its wings and back. The prions glide in formation above the water surface, their wings almost touching the waves.

Vilis paces the deck, soaking up sea, sun, and wind. Dainis periodically checks with us on the upper deck before ducking back inside out of the wind to read *Harry Potter and the Goblet of Fire* for the fourth time.

Halfway into the three-hour crossing, we lose sight of South Island, now lost in cloud and sea mist. At almost the same time, a thin, blurry darkness appears on the northern horizon.

When the *Arahura* draws closer, we see that the south shore of North Island is, like Kaikōura, a place where mountains meet the sea. Velvet-cloaked, angular slopes – many with vertical cliffs at their bases – drop into salt water. In the distance, tiny white sails of sailboats and white hulls of other ferries light the strait's dark water. High sun breaks through cloud and reveals line after line of low green peaks. The ranges of hills stretch northeast from the island's tip as though they were the cracked, tree-covered ribs of Te Ika-a-Māui – the great fish that the legendary Māori hero Māui hooked from the deep using his grandmother's jawbone baited with blood from his nose.

The *Arahura* cruises through Wellington Harbour, granting us a view of the skyscrapers at city centre. Then we're on the road again, driving north as far as Paraparaumu, where we book into a motel for our first night on North Island.

December 17

DRIZZLE MISTS roadside *nīkau* palms as we travel north from Paraparaumu on an agricultural plain scattered with towns straddling the highway. Gradually, the plain broadens into rolling farmland divided into sheep and cattle pastures and lush fields of tall corn, reminiscent of southern Ontario in central Canada. Bordered by the Ruahine Range to the east, the farming country is more verdant than the Canterbury Plain or Marlborough's dry rangeland that we drove through yesterday.

At Sanson, we head northwest, staying parallel to the coast. Past Turakina, farmland gives way to hilly rangeland that's replaced by agricultural fields near Wanganui. In the city, lush flowerpots and flowerbeds decorate storefronts and green spaces. At the city's edge, the murky Whanganui River runs broad and placid into the Tasman Sea. We lunch in a park, resting in the shade of a phoenix palm, surrounded by the buzz of cicadas, loud and mesmerizing. Nearby, tall clumps of knob-jointed bamboo elicit thrilled exclamations from Jānis, who collects a few fallen stalks to make a flute.

Heat invades the Bomb as we drive north from Wanganui. The highway twists like a snake slithering among green conical hills. Sheep and cattle graze on steep inclines littered with grey logs and charred stumps, remains of forests burned by settlers long ago. The sight is eerily familiar. We walked among other such logs and stumps in windswept pastures above Ōkuti Valley Scenic Reserve on Banks

Peninsula in early September.

Farther north, the lone hills are replaced by wrinkled ranges of hills. Dense clumps of *toetoe* (giant tussock grasses with creamy flower plumes on long stalks) grow at their bases. The car chugs upward in second gear, with the boys shooting spit balls from the back seat.

Desperate for a break from the heat and the car's confinement, we take the Raetihi exit and drive a further ten kilometres to Ōhakune and Mangawhero Forest. Beneath dark cumulus clouds, the boys romp along a rainforest trail ahead of Vilis and me. Beside us, *kāmahi* trees soar upward, their spikes of white blossoms, thin pencils of beauty among serrated leaves. *Tawa* drape long, pointed leaves from thick branches. Podocarps (conifers with fleshy berries rather than cones) rise like thick legs of giants standing in a tangle of fern fronds and thin, twisting shrub branches. I spot a *matai*, its trunk looking battered and bleeding where rounded pads of bark have fallen off.

With the aid of my tree guide, I identify *rimu*, with its scale-like leaves on drooping twigs, *miro*, with its small, flat leaves, and numerous *tōtara*, their thick trunks covered with rough, stringy bark. Vilis points to the forest. "You know those hills we drove through? Those sharp, pointy hills? Take a look at this. These hills go down sharply on either side. If you cut down this forest, you'd have those pointy hills."

Drizzle drips cooling moisture on us as we listen to the refreshing rush of a creek. We hear calls of unknown birds and breathe in dank, rich rainforest smells. The boys attempt to climb a *kiekie* vine hanging from a tree, and Vilis runs his gaze up a *matai* ensnared by thick vines that rope around its metre-thick trunk. Ferns drape the tree's branches that also offer substrate for perching lilies.

"There's a whole little ecosystem up there," Vilis points out.

I soak up information from my guidebooks and spew it out, telling Vilis and the boys that the explorer James Cook brewed beer from young *rimu* and *mānuka* twigs, and that towering trunks of *tōtara* were felled by the Māori and carved into huge war canoes, some of which could carry a hundred warriors.[16] I point out more plants, including *heketara* or tree daisy, with its oval leaves and clusters of small white flowers, and an arrow-leaved *koromiko* that resembles a dense clump of willow.[17]

My rambunctious sons barely listen. Instead, they shove handfuls of grass seeds down each other's shirts. Then Jānis smiles angelically and says, "Okay, continue."

Dainis rips out a belch and marches forward, shouting, "Hup, two, three, four! Dawdle, two, three, four! Belch, two, three, four!"

FIVE-LAYER FORESTS

New Zealand's forests are home to almost 400 plant species. In any given New Zealand forest, plants typically arrange themselves in five layers or strata. In the uppermost stratum, the gigantic podocarps such as *matai* and *rimu*, tower above all else. Tall hardwoods like *tawa* and *kāmahi* comprise a fourth layer, with canopies high above the ground. In the middle of the forest profile, tree ferns and *nīkau* palms toss fronds and leaves into the forest air, creating a subcanopy below that of the hardwoods. Shrubs like *koromiko* and tree nettle inhabit a second layer above the forest floor. Grasses, mosses, ferns, lichens, and lilies carpet the first stratum, which is the forest floor itself. Vines like clematis and supplejack penetrate upward through the layers. Epiphytic orchids, perching lilies, and many fern species sprout from tree trunks and branches, creating rich and diverse gardens in the sky.[18]

As we continue our walk, we note that the rainforest's understory is so dense, it's difficult to see past tree ferns' shaggy skirts of dead fronds and mountain cabbage trees' thick capes of leaves. "If we didn't have this path, it would be tough walking," Vilis says. We pass a tall tree with so many perching lilies, it resembles an apartment building, and another like a ladder with a lily perched on each rung. A young *rimu* stands like a maiden draped in weeping branches. Fern fronds arc into lush green curves under which I imagine gnomes hiding.

Peace settles over me. "Now this is what I came to New Zealand for," I tell Vilis and the boys. "Imagine! Just *imagine!* Maybe long ago you would have seen moas. Maybe you would have found moas right here." In this dark, thick, sheltering forest.

HOURS LATER, the few streets of Ōwhango greet us, the small village quiet on this summer's eve. "Before we go to the house, I want to show you the forest," Vilis says. He steers the station wagon onto Whakapapa Bush Road, a gravel road leading east from the village through the adjacent Ōhinetonga Scenic Reserve and downhill to the rushing, boulder-strewn Whakapapa River and, beyond the river, Tongariro Forest Conservation Area. Dark and lush in the dim light, the uncut, old-growth, native forest within the scenic reserve forms a dense wall on both sides of the narrow road. Fern and tree fern fronds curve out over the gravel.

"We'll see more of it tomorrow," Vilis promises. He turns the station wagon around and drives across the highway and a railway track to Ohoeka Street. The house we'll live in for the next month is tall and dark green, with a long, grassy yard behind it. "People call it the DOC house," Vilis tells the boys and me, "because DOC [Department of Conservation] rents it for field crews to use when they're working here. It's owned by some people who built it as a ski house."

Inside, the house is trim and modern with a vaulted ceiling over a spacious living room lined by a wall of windows. An extension off the house holds a hot tub. Vilis introduces the boys and me to Tala, who traps stoats for Andrea Byrom, his colleague in Landcare Research's Vertebrate Pest Management Unit. Slender and blond, Tala is wrapped in a tie-died skirt. She welcomes us in a slippery North Island accent that leaves me wondering if I caught what she said.

Vilis and I carry our gear up to a bedroom on the second floor. The boys spread their sleeping bags on cushion-covered benches set against the living room's glass wall. In the night, rain pours down, its drumbeat loud and insistent on the metal roof over our heads.

December 18

TWENTY KILOMETRES north of Ōwhango, heat bounces off the walls and streets of Taumarunui. Known as the "Heart of the King Country," this town was one of the last locations Europeans settled in the Central North Island.[19] The town is slow and has a laid-back feel about it, as though its residents breathe a different air from that of South Island. I feel a connection with a different past, one that existed long before Canterbury's neatly walled gardens and precise hedges. Here, Māori walk the streets. One – a slim, warm-skinned teen in cut-offs and bare feet – with quick, graceful steps claims ownership of the sidewalk.

We stock up on groceries and petrol and buy four motorcycle helmets. Then Vilis loads a Yamaha quad he's arranged to rent for a month onto a trailer behind the car.

On our return to Ōwhango, Vilis gives me a quad-driving lesson. He's on the rented Yamaha, and I'm on a Honda quad on loan from the Landcare Research branch in Palmerston North. He tells me, "When you're driving uphill, you lean forward, and when you're driving downhill, you lean back."

"Like riding a horse," I say.

"Yeah." He drives slowly downhill on Whakapapa Bush Road, and I follow. Dainis and Jānis saunter beside us along the gravel road. My helmet is heavy, and its thick padding muffles my hearing. Vilis stops frequently to instruct me, and then finally says, "All right. Let's try going faster." The Honda roars when I open its throttle. Gravel kicks up from beneath its wheels. I feel a heady sense of power over this earth dragon.

AFTER SUPPER, Tala provides us with a guided tour of Ōwhango. Formerly a lumber-mill town, Ōwhango now bases its economy on tourism. Tala shows us the dairy, ski shop, garage, primary school, and lastly, the domain, a recreation park that's an expanse of grassy playing fields. The domain also features a children's playground and a pair of tennis courts hidden from unsuspecting eyes by trees. The courts are like no others I've seen. Their nets sag above chipped, cracked concrete pads. Blackberries and shrubs poke through a chain link fence that appears to be fighting a losing battle with forest giants that tower ten times as high beside it. A bellbird's voice spills into the evening air; its clear, ringing notes announce the arrival of invaders, or perhaps...of guests.

Tala tells us that many of the locals hunt in Tongariro Forest, often using spotlights.

"They're allowed to spotlight [jack]?" I ask in surprise.

She tosses her blond hair. "Well, everything they hunt is a pest, so no one cares how they do it."

Of course. I'd momentarily forgotten that all the wild mammals in New Zealand (except for two native bat species) are descendants of non-native mammals introduced to this country by explorers, colonists, sportsmen, and farmers. Many of those mammals are destructive pests that pose major threats to native ecosystems.

December 19

THE SHADOWED arboreal giants of Ōhinetonga Scenic Reserve flash past while Vilis and I, with the boys seated behind us on the quads, drive Whakapapa Bush Road downhill to Whakapapa River.

WHAKAPAPA RIVER

Beyond a cement bridge, the road becomes the 42 Traverse, named for the original State Forest 42. A forty-six-kilometre multi-use track that crosses Tongariro Forest Conservation Area, the 42 Traverse is a mecca for mountain bikers and quad enthusiasts. It's also "Main Street" for the stoat research project. Other tracks branch off it: Water Supply Road, Mud Track, Mariner's Track, Top Track,

Climo's Track. All were logging roads until concern for the forest prompted local citizens to demand its protection which eventually led to the establishment of the conservation area.[20]

A short distance beyond the bridge, Vilis pulls off the track onto the flat bed of a small, abandoned quarry. I stop the Honda beside him. The quarry's bed is criss-crossed with quad tracks. Its rear wall is a sheer, bullet-pocked rock face topped by shrubs and scattered trees. "This is an old pumice quarry," Vilis tells the boys and me. "There's pumice all over the place here, from old volcanic eruptions."

AT THE PUMICE QUARRY NEAR WHAKAPAPA RIVER

He and Jānis roar back onto the track, and I follow, with Dainis seated behind me. Our task today is to check the stoat traps already set along the 42 Traverse, radio-collar any new stoats caught, and check tracking tunnels that had previously been set to collect stoat tracks in order to determine where to set more traps.

For two kilometres past the quarry, the 42 Traverse is broad and well-maintained. The forest beside it is thick with trees, vines, and ferns. This is habitat for brown kiwi, New Zealand's nocturnal, long-beaked mascot. In Ōwhango, we've heard high-pitched kiwi cries issuing from the scenic reserve after dusk. Now I try to envision the dumpy, flightless birds stalking through the night, probing with their beaks among fallen fern fronds in this forest.

FIVE KINDS OF KIWI

New Zealand forests are home to five kiwi species, the largest of which is the great spotted kiwi of northern South Island. The little spotted kiwi, smallest of all kiwi and a target for stoats even in adult life, became extinct in the wild on the North Island mainland, but that was after successful introduction to Kapiti Island. On the smaller island, the population flourished, allowing translocations to several other predator-free, offshore islands and to Wellington's Zealandia Sanctuary. *Tokoeka* live on South Island and Stewart Island (at the southern end of South Island). Stewart Island *tokoeka* are unusual in that they are active during daylight. Haast *tokoeka*, which live in harsh, mountainous terrain in far south and southwest South Island, are severely endangered, with only 400 birds remaining (stoats being the main killers). Soft-feathered *rowi* inhabit forests in the Ōkārito region of the South Island's West Coast. The brown kiwi, most familiar of all kiwi species, lives in the wild only on North Island.[21]

Orange ribbons of flagging tape labelled with black numbers cue us to the presence of traps or tracking tunnels set within the dense rainforest. At the first few of these flags, Vilis mentors the boys and me on to how to search for the traps and tracking tunnels, which are set metres back from the trail and camouflaged with mosses or fallen tree fern fronds. "Look for the box shape," he tells us. "Sometimes you'll only see the end of it."

Each trap is a narrow wooden box about sixty centimetres long with a Plexiglas wall at one end and a trip-door at the other. The trap rests on the forest floor with its trip-door open and facing the trail for easy monitoring. "Once you find the trap, you have to check whether the door has been tripped," Vilis tells the boys and me, "and if it has, see whether or not there's an animal in it." He lifts a trap and swings it around to show us the Plexiglas end, through which we see a large tuft of synthetic bedding. "If there's a stoat in the trap, you'll either see it moving around or feel its movements. If there is one, you just leave it and come and tell me, then I'll collar it."

The tracking tunnels look like pale brown boxes without ends. Square in cross-section, they're also about sixty centimetres long and were cut from corrugated plastic tree protectors. Within each tunnel, a piece of white corrugated plastic lines the floor. A central panel of the white plastic is painted with a mixture of paraffin oil and powdered charcoal. Narrow sheets of white paper are tacked to the plastic on both sides of the central panel. "When a stoat, rat, or mouse enters a tunnel, it has to step on the charcoal to get to the peanut butter bait," Vilis explains, holding up a tunnel. "When it leaves the tunnel, its footprints show up on the paper as black tracks we can identify."

The boys and I listen carefully and learn how to replace bait and bedding in the traps when necessary, and how to change papers in the tracking tunnels. Dainis and Jānis are grossed out by the bits of chopped lab mice used as stoat bait, but otherwise are keen to assist.

As we proceed from flag to flag, the track narrows beyond Water Supply Road. Cautiously, I guide the Honda across a sharply-angled, rolling outcrop of bedrock, where Dainis and I are slapped and cut by the curved, slicing leaf edges of *toetoe* growing in clumps beside the track.

Tala roars up on her Honda quad to tell Vilis she's trapped a stoat. Thrilled, we speed past dense walls of forest, open vistas chaotic with lush vegetation, and a waterfall that spills down a black wall edged with graceful ferns. My heart pounds as we plunge downhill into Little Mako Stream and wade the quads across Big Mako Stream (more a river than a stream). On the far side of the Big Mako, Tala takes a dauntingly steep hill fast, leaning far over her quad's front wheels. Vilis, noting my hesitation, drives the Honda up while Dainis and I walk to the top.

When we catch up with Tala, it's to discover that the stoat she's trapped isn't a new animal. Instead, it's Sarah, a young male – not a female as the name suggests. Tala's a little chagrined, but the ear-tagged stoat is gorgeous. Long and lean with a rich brown pelage, white belly, and black-tipped tail, it peers inquisitively through the Plexiglas trap end, eyes bright in a classic, bullet-shaped weasel head.

STOAT IN TRAP

Although stoats (*Mustela erminea*) like Sarah are small and have short legs, they're highly mobile and are adept at climbing trees in pursuit of prey. Here in New Zealand, they occur in any habitat where they can find food and den sites. Those habitats include rainforests like Tongariro Forest, other native forests, grasslands, and exotic plantations. Because stoats have a high metabolic rate, they feed up to six times a day, posing a huge threat to native birds. Stoats also have a high reproductive rate, with females producing an average of six young per litter.[22] As a result of these traits, stoats could be classified as a "perfect storm" invasive species.

> ### The Stoat Invasion
> In 1884, frustrated New Zealand farmers wanting to control rabbits that were overgrazing pastures and causing soil erosion released hundreds of stoats on farmland in the South Island provinces of Canterbury, Otago, Fiordland, and Marlborough, and in North Island's Wairarapa District. This happened despite warnings given by prominent New Zealand naturalists that such introductions could have disastrous negative impacts on native ecosystems. Within ten years of their introduction, it was obvious that stoats were not controlling rabbit populations. Further evidence showed that stoats had spread far from their release sites and were eating native birds. In the 1930s, New Zealand's government retracted legislation protecting stoats, and instead set bounties on them.[23]

It's thought that young stoats, like the male Sarah, may disperse widely in order to find places where they can establish territories of their own. At sites where the Department of Conservation has eliminated resident stoats, other stoats (mostly juveniles) often re-invade.[24] It's not known how far young stoats disperse, but that's an important consideration when devising a plan to keep stoats away from vulnerable birds like kiwi, blue ducks (*whio*), and New Zealand's critically endangered flightless parrot, the *kākāpō*. And this is Vilis's research project: to investigate how far juvenile stoats disperse. Once that's known, it will help Landcare Research and the Department of Conservation determine how large an area must be cleared of stoats in order to keep it stoat-free.

Vilis shows Sarah off to the boys, who radiate excitement.

I've watched my husband anaesthetize and radio-collar weasels in Canada's Northwest Territories, so allow myself to be lured away from the stoat by a striking bird song that consists of upward-sliding split notes followed by downward-sliding tones. Eventually, I attribute the song to a shining cuckoo, a small, chunky forest bird with a metallic green back and green bars across its face, neck, and belly. Like other cuckoos, the shining cuckoo is a nest parasite. It lays its eggs in the nests of other bird species, to be hatched and raised by unsuspecting avian foster parents. Happily, I record another "lifer" in my small notebook, one of half a dozen I've filled with observations about New Zealand.

Vilis calls to me after they release Sarah, and we mount our quads to resume checking traps and tracking tunnels on the west end of the 42 Traverse. Tala will check the remaining traps on the east end and then on Top Track. Top Track twists and climbs away from the 42 Traverse onto a ridge of steep hills bordering Waione Stream, before angling westward and descending back to the main track via Mud Track or "downhill-only" Climo's Track. I ease the Honda down the steep hill to the Big Mako and, once we're across the river, Dainis and I join Vilis and Jānis for a bag lunch within Tongariro Forest.

On the shaded forest floor, dead fern fronds form a rusty-beige mattress. Mosses and a collage of ferns cover tree fern trunks. The filmy fern is so pale and thin, it's almost translucent. The boys tug on vines, kick stones, and knock over dead tree fern trunks as they explore their new environment. "I'm really glad we came to the

North Island!" Jānis exclaims.

LUNCH IN TONGARIRO FOREST

When we finish checking traps and tunnels on the 42 Traverse, we turn off the track onto Water Supply Road. A steep, rough road of bedrock and broken stone that's wider and easier to navigate than most of the 42 Traverse we've just driven, Water Supply Road leads past the bottom end of Mud Track, on which two traps are located. As we drive up the road, which frequently nears the edge of a sharp drop-off, we pause several times to gaze at long views of steep-sided hills cloaked with regenerating forest.

With Jānis seated behind him, Vilis turns onto Mud Track and steers his quad into a gaping mudhole. The Yamaha tilts alarmingly as it lurches out of the hole onto a deeply rutted track. Jānis grins.

I slam on the Honda's brakes, filled with trepidation at the thought of driving into that enormous hole. Dainis and I look at each other. He hops off the Honda, saying, "I'm going to walk." I follow suit, and he and I walk in on Mud Track to check our last assigned trap before returning to the Honda.

VIEW FROM WATER SUPPLY ROAD

In mid-afternoon, with our work completed, we return to the green house. My shoulders ache from wrestling with the quad, and I realize that although I spent five hours driving through the forest, I actually spent very little time *in* the forest.

After supper, Jānis and I hunt for parrots in Ōwhango's domain and are rewarded with a sighting of an eastern rosella. The slim Australian parrot wings across a grassy playing field, its head scarlet, its long tail green, its back patterned with black and yellow, and its wings the rich dark blue of oncoming night.

December 20

AT 8:30 A.M., we're on the 42 Traverse, adding traps to tracking tunnel sites that lack them. We also place tracking tunnels halfway between existing tunnels to increase the chances of stoats encountering them within their home ranges of about a square kilometre. In order to determine how far juvenile stoats disperse, Vilis must radio-collar young animals, then use a radio-telemetry receiver and antenna to obtain locations for them. Once he has a collection of locations for a given stoat, he can determine how far it has dispersed.

Beyond trap 37A, we turn the quads onto overgrown Mariner's Track and drive past several grassy clearings dotted with cabbage trees, an unusual habitat within the overall expanse of the forest. Narrow, sharp *toetoe* leaves cut our hands, and shrub branches whip our faces.

ON MARINER'S TRACK

I follow Vilis up and down steep hills and pause before tackling quad-swallowing mudholes. My quad-driving skills are improving by leaps and bounds. When confronted by a massive hole spanning the track, Vilis skirts its edge and almost tips himself and Dainis into the mud. I drive straight into the hole and barely climb out of it, with Jānis and I clinging to the fighting Honda while muddy water gushes out of the hole and down the hill. Farther along the track, Vilis orders Dainis off the Yamaha before he roars into another deep hole and gets mired in its muck. He manages to fight his way out backward, then skirts the hole. After commanding Jānis to climb off the Honda, I do the same.

Our research day is long and intense, yet the boys never complain. The excitement of being quad cowboys compensates for the repetitiveness of checking traps and tracking tunnels. Today, we're not rewarded with a captured stoat.

Back at the house, tea plus "pudding" of peaches and coconut cream prepared by Tala tastes incredibly delicious. We thank her profusely, and afterward stroll with her through the village. At the sound of a siren, she abandons us, sprints back to the house, and leaps on her motorcycle to assume her role as a volunteer fire fighter. Darkness arrives before she returns, and the wild cries of kiwi echo in the night.

December 21

VILIS USES a hatchet to chop frozen white lab mice into halves for stoat bait, then drops the truncated bodies into two plastic bags. He grins and hands me a bag. "Here you go."

I gingerly accept the bag, with its gruesome contents, and he and I mount the quads with the boys behind us. As on our first work day, Dainis rides with me. The boys will alternate between Vilis and me so they have equal time with each parent. We race downhill on Whakapapa Bush Road, then slow our pace past the river as we split up to check odd and even traps on the 42 Traverse.

This is the first time Dainis and I have worked on our own. We strain to spot the correct flags and traps. Some traps are easy to find, but others are hidden beneath their fern or moss camouflage.

When we locate a trap, I reach inside with a gloved hand to remove the old bait, which invariably writhes with maggots and stinks in the heat. At the first trap, Dainis grimaces and blurts, "*Eee-ew!* That is *so* gross!" I replace the slimy, disintegrating bait with one of the frozen mouse halves that don't stay frozen as long as I'd like. Dainis starts the quad for me and we roar past Vilis and Jānis to check our next trap. By noon, the remaining soft, oozing mouse half-bodies in the plastic bag have attracted a swarm of flies that buzz along behind the quad.

After completing trap checks, we rendezvous at the pumice quarry where Vilis says, "I've got something to show you." We leave the quads in the quarry and climb one of two heavily eroded pumice tracks that lead into the forest. Vilis shows us a clearing bordered by towering trees and groves of tree ferns. He spreads his arms. "Isn't this the perfect camping spot?" Charmed by the site's serenity, we decide to camp here on Christmas Eve, only three days away.

In the forest past the clearing, Vilis and I set seven tracking tunnels, using bits of leftover, cut-up-mouse bait. The boys romp among the tree ferns beside us, and Dainis discovers a sagging curve of vine, which he uses as a swing.

After the tunnels are set, we hike out to the quads, and Vilis and Jānis head off to obtain GPS (Global Positioning System) locations for the new traps and tunnels we set yesterday. The GPS locations will allow Vilis to plot all the trap and tunnel locations on a topographical map of Tongariro Forest Conservation Area he has on his laptop.

Dainis and I return to the house, where I prepare a midday meal of leftover stir-fry and rice, to which I add chopped leftover chicken. After Vilis and Jānis return, the four of us pick away at my improvised casserole. Belatedly, I realize that the meal resembles stoat bait that's been decomposing under a hot sun.

"The rice grains look like maggots, don't they?" I say.

"Yeah," Dainis agrees, distaste in his expression.

"And the bits of chicken could be slimy chunks of disintegrating mouse," Vilis adds.

The meal's only saving grace is that it doesn't stink.

After eating the less-than-appealing casserole, we drive to Taumarunui for supplies. The town is baking. Heat radiates from sidewalks and streets traversed by barefoot Māori residents. While Vilis buys bricks and boards to build shelves to hold shoes, books, and miscellaneous research supplies, I spot mynas – introduced Asian songbirds with glossy black heads and pale brown bodies – in yards and on the roof of Mitre 10 Hardware.

On our return to Ōwhango, Tala has another delicious tea ready: lasagne, root vegetables, and salad. After the meal, Vilis constructs his shelves, and we unpack boxes of research materials that arrived by mail yesterday, although one box is missing.

"I like the way this is a community forest," Vilis tells Tala while he works. "I know the quads wreck the trails, but I like that everyone uses it. It's not owned by the government and managed, or owned by some logging company that can decide to clear-cut it. It's like when I was at Ten Man Hut [on his last visit in November]. If there's something that needs repairs, someone writes it in the book there, and the next person coming in brings what's needed and fixes it."

It was this same community spirit that saved Tongariro Forest. After seventy-five years of logging, the cutting that had supplied forty-three mills ended in 1978 due to lack of timber. Local groups campaigned against New Zealand Forest Service's plan to turn the land over to farming and exotic pine plantations. Instead, the groups wanted to protect the forest to conserve it, offer recreation opportunities, and protect Ōwhango's water supply. In 1987, the Department of Conservation assumed responsibility for the forest, which encloses one of this country's five kiwi sanctuaries.[25] Now Tongariro Forest Conservation Area is used by hunters and scientists, quad enthusiasts and cyclists.

And here, wild kiwi screams still pierce the night.

DAINIS ON A VINE SWING

December 22

BEFORE 8:00 A.M., we're in the field. Vilis, Jānis, and Tala will check and close traps for the Christmas holiday weekend while Dainis and I set more tracking tunnels above the pumice quarry. So far, with the exception of the masculine Sarah, the stoat traps have been empty. This is good news for the forest's vulnerable kiwi, but bad news for Vilis's research project.

I park the Honda at the pumice quarry, and Dainis and I climb the steeper of the two tracks to set twenty tracking tunnels, hoping some of them will capture stoat sign. Above the quarry, the forest is like dusk and dawn, its dense, shady thickets interspersed with grassy clearings. Dainis and I discover a secluded waterfall tumbling down a rock bank and name it "Hidden Waterfall." A narrow stream at the foot of the falls passes silently beneath a footbridge constructed from tree fern trunks.

Farther on, in open woodland, we slip inside a walled and roofed viewing shelter labelled "DANGEROUS LOOKOUT," which is perched at the edge of a sheer cliff bordering Whakapapa River. From the lookout, the view is all down to the cliff, to the water rushing at its base, and beyond the river, to open green fields and a farmhouse set against a backdrop of forest. Carefully, Dainis and I exit the lookout and continue inspecting the main track and its side trails in an effort to find sites to set five remaining tunnels.

The track, like the rest we've encountered, is pitted with mudholes. Some are small and undoubtedly navigable on a quad; some are intimidating in size and are water-filled, giving no indication as to their depth. Today, I'm happy to be on foot.

"This is peaceful," Dainis comments.

"Yes. We can hear the birds." For a birder, this is a definite plus.

Later, Dainis adds, somewhat surprisingly, "This is better than riding on the back of a quad."

Unable to locate any additional suitable tracking tunnel sites along the trails (the criteria being that the site must be forested and spaced at least thirty metres from other tunnels), we return to the pumice quarry and coincidentally meet Vilis and Jānis. Dainis tells them about Hidden Waterfall and the lookout, and we all hike the eroded pumice track up into the forest, where Dainis and I lead Vilis and Jānis to these discoveries.

While we stroll, Vilis nods toward Jānis. "He's becoming a real petrol-head."

Jānis grins at the reference to his love for quadding.

I look around at the rich, cluttered forest, with its trees towering high above us, its tangled vines, and its floor littered with rusty tree fern fronds. "When we return to Canada, I think we'll find Canadian forests austere," I say.

"Yes," Vilis agrees.

"What does that mean?" Jānis asks.

"Not lush like these." I love the forests surrounding our home in Nova Scotia, with their majestic white pines, gorgeous paper birches, and stately hemlocks, but they don't have the tree-ferns, vines, and variety of parasitic plants that clutter Tongariro Forest.

We return to the DOC house, and in early afternoon place packs and a cooler of food in the station wagon – preparations for a short excursion to Lake Taupō. There, we'll visit Chris Morse, a Landcare Research technician from Lincoln who invited us to spend a night at his family's bach on Kuratau Spit, sixty-five kilometres northeast of Ōwhango. Jānis bounces with joy before he climbs into the car. "I'm very glad we came to the North Island," he tells Vilis and me. "It's been a lot of fun so far."

Near Taumarunui, we turn east toward Lake Taupō and trace knife-edge hills, the Hauhungaroa Ranges. The Whanganui River, which I once thought misspelled, runs parallel to the highway for a time. Sheep, velvet-antlered deer, and horses seek the shade of trees on hills bordering the river. To the southeast, three volcanoes on the Central Volcanic Plateau push into the sky. The northernmost, Tongariro, is an elegant upsweep of massive slopes truncated by a shattered peak. Ngāuruhoe is a slim cone, half hidden behind Tongariro. Ruapehu towers behind the others, its cusped peak covered with snow.

As the Bomb climbs into the hills, I spot introduced tamarack trees growing by the roadside, and a monkey puzzle tree with tail-like branches hanging to the ground, each with dense spirals of triangular leaves. Within Waituhi-Kuratau Scenic Reserve, hillside forests are thick with tree ferns, and two feral goats scamper across the highway. Halfway to Kuratau Spit, we pause at Waituhi Lookout and spot the classic volcanic cone of Taranaki (also called Mount Egmont), far to the west. On a road map, the volcano protrudes from the mainland like a huge bud reminiscent of Banks Peninsula. Other smaller volcanic cones pimple the landscape.

Farms lie at the base of the lookout's hills, and one field displays large square bales wrapped in blue plastic. "The houses certainly aren't as fancy here as in Canterbury," Vilis notes, no doubt recalling the modern cement-block Cantabrian homes with their metal or clay-tiled roofs. "They would look right at home in Nova Scotia. Your basic wood frame." As we resume our eastward journey, the highway becomes a tunnel sliced into the forest. The tunnel's floor is grey pavement; its walls, green trees; and its roof, a blue sky soaring high overhead and sailed by wayward rafts of cloud.

At Kuratau Spit, we're welcomed by Chris and his parents. Their bach is a plain, flat-topped white cabin that shares a grassy, tree-shaded yard with outbuildings. It faces Lake Taupō, New Zealand's largest inland water body, which covers an area of 616 square kilometres and is up to 186 metres deep.[26] Lightweight pumice stones riddled with holes litter the lakeshore. Dainis nonchalantly balances a large one on three fingertips. We toss others onto the water and watch them float.

The lake's white-capped surface appears invitingly blue beneath the hot December sun. However, when we plunge in for a pre-Christmas dip, we discover the water is much colder than it looks. Chris offers Jānis the use of his kayak, and a few minutes later, my nine-year-old is paddling over white-laced waves whose beauty disguises scars of two of the earth's most violent volcanic events.

DAINIS AND PUMICE AT LAKE TAUPŌ

JĀNIS KAYAKING ON LAKE TAUPŌ

According to the New Zealand Geothermal Association, "This zone is the result of a million years of some of the most violent volcanic action recorded on this planet."[27] Long before Polynesian explorers reached the shores of Aotearoa (the Māori name for New Zealand), a massive volcanic explosion located where Lake Taupō now lies blasted unimaginable volumes of lava and ash over the North Island landscape. Called the Ōruanui eruption, this geological incident of 26 500 years ago created 500 cubic kilometres of pumice and ash and 300 cubic kilometres of ignimbrite, a volcanic rock composed of welded pumice and glass shards. The eruption was so explosive, it blew the volcanic cone to bits and caused the ground under it to collapse, forming a caldera that subsequently filled with water.[28]

In 186 A.D., while Marcus Aurelius fought the barbarian hordes in Europe to extend the Roman Empire, but still hundreds of years before humans set foot on these islands, history more or less repeated itself in the form of the Taupō eruption. That eruption again blasted a volcano on this site to smithereens in what geologists describe as the largest and most violent volcanic eruption of the past 5 000 years. Heard as far away as China, the Taupō eruption blasted nine cubic kilometres of pumice fifty kilometres into the air and once again resulted in the formation of a collapsed volcano.[29]

While Chris's mother and I relax in lawn chairs on the beach, she tells me of pockets of heated water in the lake, of fishermen lost to abrupt drop-offs in the bottom, and of the fallout from one of Ruapehu's eruptions. "It was in 1995. There was ash covering everything. Houses. Cars. It made a terrible mess of everything."

Central North Island perches on dangerously thin ground. Ruapehu spits ashes onto human creations, and beneath Lake

Taupō's brilliant blue waters, a giant, collapsed volcano slumbers and spews steam from vents in hills bordering the water. The caldera has been quiet for nearly two millennia, but it's definitely not dead.

Throughout the evening, it becomes apparent that our host loves children. Dark-haired and tanned, Chris entertains his nieces and wee nephew, as well as Dainis and Jānis. He instigates a game of Frisbee, helps to inflate a silvery raft, gives Dainis a kayaking lesson, leads a gaggle of us on an after-barbecue stroll, and fries up a feast of pancakes for a late bedtime snack. His generous hospitality fills us, far from home, with a warm sense of family.

December 23

IN THE silence of early morn, I creep from an upper bunk in the bach out into the day before Christmas Eve, in a setting far removed from a Canadian winter. For an hour and a half, in sunshine and light breezes, I explore a reserve beside vast Lake Taupō. Two dozen bird species lead me on. I watch a blackish-brown *tūī*, with white balls of feathers *(poi)* hanging from its chin, chase a starling. Several fantails coyly spread their white-and-black tails. I spot the first little black shag I've seen, its feathers glossed with a green sheen.

When I return to the bach, I join Chris and my family for a quiet breakfast, after which Chris ferries the boys to the mouth of nearby Kuratau River in a motorboat while Vilis and I enjoy a stroll along the pumice sand to where the boat waits. It's good for our kids to have a little adventure with Chris on their own.

Vilis and I scramble into the boat, and Chris motors up the river, towing his kayak. The river has a single channel of deep water flowing past shores crowded with shrubs, grasses, and trees. In the forest alongside the river, bellbirds celebrate the new day with serene, joyous tones. A shining cuckoo voices its slur-up, slur-down call, and kingfishers chatter as they flash blue-green between riverside trees.

Chris steers the motorboat near shore and supervises while Dainis and Jānis each have a go at paddling the kayak downstream. Then he offers Vilis and me a turn. My brief excursion is delightful and uneventful, but Vilis capsizes the kayak while climbing into it. His startled, soaked reappearance after his dunking sends Chris into gales of laughter. "Sorry, Vilis," he apologizes moments later, once again the perfect host.

IN EARLY afternoon, we bid farewell to Chris and his family and drive south to Lake Rotopounamu, where gigantic rainforest trees loom over us as we stroll a track around the small, circular lake. The silhouettes of the trees' canopies against the bright sky aren't neat and leafy; rather, they're wild with a clutter of parasitic plants that perch on branches like alien porcupines sprouting long, curving leaf-quills. Shrubs crowd into the track, and thick vines lean like slim trunks hung from the treetops. Ferns and fungi abound. One of the latter is a shelf fungus resembling small, rumpled hides of thick white leather.

Where the trail nears the lakeshore, we explore a pumice-sand beach. The boys kick at clods of foam stranded on the beach while grey ducks float offshore. Dainis stoops to collect handfuls of foam, and then laughs as he shapes the foam into a beard and attaches it to his chin. When we re-enter the forest, the circle track soon leads us beneath forest giants again. Their untidy mop-heads of parasitic plants seem to wave their leaves at us in cheeky goodbyes.

Hours later, we return to Ōwhango and unpack from our excursion. Although the season seems wrong, and the temperature definitely *feels* wrong, the excitement of this particular time in December fills the house with delicious anticipation. Tomorrow is Christmas Eve.

THIS DARK SHELTERING FOREST 71

December 24

RAIN DRIPS a gentle curtain while we search for a young tree fern to serve as our Christmas tree. We've seen fences built of tree fern trunks, some of which sprouted new fronds, so we plan to return our celebration fern to the forest following Christmas, with the hope that it will survive a transplant. We find the perfect shape in a young specimen with a short trunk and a dozen soaring, beautifully curved fronds. Vilis cuts it off near its base with a machete, and we carefully place it in our station wagon.

CHRISTMAS TREE FERN

"I see you've got yourselves a *ponga*," Tala tells us on our return, and then hurries upstairs to her bedroom. Moments later, she returns to the living room, where Vilis and I have erected the tree fern in a pan of water. She opens a bag. "If you want to decorate it, I've got a few things."

In minutes, the tree fern glimmers with tinsel, strings of gold beads, and small red wooden apples, one for each frond. It's beautiful! As the afternoon passes, we secretively slide colourfully wrapped boxes beneath the curving fronds, and Tala plays Christmas carols on her flute and recorder.

"Now, I really miss our piano," Jānis mourns, but his spirits brighten as he and Dainis punch holes into DB Draught beer cans to improvise candle-lanterns. This is in preparation for our Christmas Eve campout. Under Vilis's direction, the boys insert candles into the cans and tie sturdy strings to the can lids. In early evening, we pack the candle-lanterns, our tent, rain gear, bedding, hot chocolate, and snacks and load them into the car, then drive to the pumice quarry.

Our laughter spills into the drizzle as we walk up one of the eroded pumice tracks leading from the quarry, and then erect our tent beneath tall trees at the forest's edge. The tent door faces a view of the grassy clearing bordered by *whēkī* so lush and robust, the sturdy tree-ferns resemble tousle-headed women attired in layered gowns.

WHĒKĪ AT OUR CHRISTMAS EVE CAMPSITE

A New Zealand robin as grey as the encroaching dusk visits our campsite while Vilis and the boys tie candle-lanterns to shrub branches in front of the tent and light the candles. Then we lounge within our shelter, sipping hot chocolate and munching chippies while Vilis reads aloud from Mona Anderson's *A River Rules My Life*, the memoir of a South Island sheep rancher's wife. Beyond the open tent door, punctured beer cans toss shards of bright light into the warm night of Christmas Eve.

December 25

BACK AT the house, we enjoy a soak in the hot tub and, afterward, meet Tala's husband Bill, who arrived following our departure from the house last evening. As slim and blond as Tala, he radiates dynamic energy. The six of us share a brunch of pancakes fried by Vilis and topped with fruit, maple syrup, and whipped cream. Then Tala and Bill motorcycle off on a summer vacation, and my family opens gifts while rain, not snow, falls from the sky on Christmas Day.

December 26

IT'S BACK to fieldwork on this Boxing Day morning. The quad is as loud as I remember, and the motorcycle helmet as heavy. Cloud bellies sag into the forest, and rain-soaked plants slap water onto Dainis's and my rain coats and pants. Moisture drips down our necks when we push past fern fronds and tree branches to find and set stoat traps as far as 37A on the 42 Traverse. Vilis and Jānis have driven on to open traps on the 42 Traverse's far reaches and on Top Track. Then they'll locate the two radio-collared stoats Tala caught before we arrived in Ōwhango, Sarah and Shiraz.

My older son and I soon develop a routine. At each trap, I insert fresh mouse bait I chopped this morning, after which Dainis adds a loose ball of clean synthetic batting for bedding. Then I set the trap, balancing the treadle for an accurate response – not so light a trigger that the trap will be tripped by the slight jolt of rain or a falling twig, but not so heavy that it won't be tripped by the weight of a stoat. Dainis starts the quad while I gently place a dead fern frond or a handful of leaves atop the trap to disguise its appearance.

Once Dainis and I have set our assigned traps on the 42 Traverse, I drive the Honda up steep, rocky Water Supply Road. The view is all mist and rain-washed hills, or from a different height, vivid green farmland stretching toward the horizon. We pause often to gaze out over the landscape then walk in along Mud Track to set the two traps near the track's lower end.

Stoats are so few in Tongariro Forest. Far fewer than we expected. The tracking tunnels reveal mostly rat and mouse tracks, and the stoat capture frequency is extremely low. I've sensed Vilis's frustration. His research hinges on these four weeks. Given that Landcare had already initiated a stoat project here, he assumed there would be enough animals to gather the necessary data to determine how far juvenile stoats disperse. It appears that might not be the case.

After we return to the tall green house in early afternoon, Dainis begins constructing forty tracking tunnels of his own. He'll use them to collect small mammal tracks in four habitats within the old-growth native forest in Ōhinetonga Scenic Reserve, a project designed to earn him the Individual Specialty badge in Scouting.

IN LATE afternoon, I wash an entire load of laundry by hand. It's the first time I've done this since I scrubbed clothes while kneeling on tundra at Alexandra Fiord in Canada's High Arctic. There, I rinsed the clothes in a net bag I cast into an ice-cold, glacier-fed river. That was twenty years ago. Now, as my rubber-gloved fingers work out sweat, dirt, and stains, I feel myself slipping back into field biologist mode, where life seems closer to the earth.

AFTER VILIS and Dainis return from the forest, I ask Vilis, "Did DOC know how few stoats there are here when they suggested this site for the project?"

He shakes his head. "It's more like they know stoats prey on kiwi, so set up the stoat project where they have this kiwi project." Part of Tongariro Forest Conservation Area is a national kiwi sanctuary where the Department of Conservation controls predators in order to protect the local brown kiwi population.[30]

"Have you considered the possibility of doing your project somewhere else, somewhere where you know there are lots of stoats?" I ask.

"No, but I will. Of course, that would mean living somewhere else for six weeks." He reflects. "But that is a possibility. I'll have to think about it."

With less than six months remaining of our time in New Zealand, organizing a field study in a different locale would be a major undertaking.

December 27

TODAY, JĀNIS and I return from the forest drenched, shivering, and ravenous after five hours of checking empty traps and changing tracking tunnel papers in steady rain. I make grilled cheese sandwiches for a late midday meal. Beside me, Jānis is almost asleep at the table, his chin in his hand. After we wolf down the hot sandwiches, I quickly set out my data book and the collected tracking papers to dry. Then we luxuriate in the hot tub.

Afternoon slides by. I record more of our New Zealand

adventures on the laptop while Jānis reads and plays with a remote-controlled truck he received as a Christmas gift.

In mid-afternoon, Vilis and Dainis return from the forest. Dainis grins as he stands at the glass patio door, his dripping raincoat and pants decorated with *toetoe* seeds.

"Hi, there, quad cowboy," I greet him when he steps inside. "How did it go?"

"Pretty good, but there was one place I really didn't like." He describes a section of Top Track pitted with eroded holes. "It was really ugly."

"It was," Vilis agrees as he and the boys slip into the hot tub to warm up. "This is sure a decadent field station," he calls to me. "And it sure feels like rainforest out there today."

The house is draped with soggy clothes, the residue of our fieldwork. Outdoors, the clothes I washed and hung on a backyard clothesline yesterday hang limp and sodden. Today is the fourth straight day of rain and a mockery of my laundering efforts.

Later, Vilis shows me a topographical map of the stoat research project study area on the laptop. The screen shows all the tracks and the locations of every trap and tracking tunnel.

"I wonder if I should try the other track to get back from Ten Man Hut to see if it's worth setting tunnels along it," he muses. The "other track" links the west end of Top Track with the top of Climo's Track and then Mud Track and Water Supply Road. "The rest of the study site is covered, where accessible by quad. The only other option is walking in on some of the tracks inaccessible to vehicles." Finally, he decides, "I'll give it a try tomorrow."

As I store the tracking papers I set out to dry earlier, Vilis suggests, "Why don't you use Tala's field book tomorrow? It has waterproof pages."

I chuckle. "Mine certainly doesn't. It'll be okay, if it doesn't rain."

Overhearing our conversation, Dainis tosses me a dry look. "But it *will* rain. This is New Zealand."

December 28

AFTER TRANSPLANTING our Christmas fern, Vilis gazes at the lush rainforest surrounding us and sighs. "I sure do like this forest. I just love being out in it."

"For the tree fern's sake, I hope it rains today," I say, laughing, "but not until after everyone's home."

My wish to return home first is not to be. Drizzle and then rain spill down onto Tongariro Forest. The trees drip water, and sodden ferns arch wide over Whakapapa Bush Road. Shrub branches and *toetoe* seed heads slap Dainis's and my coats as we ride the Honda over tracks crowded by encroaching vegetation. Again, all our assigned traps are empty.

As we zip homeward, I slow down for short, difficult sections of track, my least favourite being a humped and rolling, sharply-angled bedrock outcrop hidden behind a curve in the track and a dive down through overhanging branches. At what the stoat crew calls Waterfall Bridge, Dainis and I pause for a few minutes to enjoy the gentle waterfall's pretty spill of white water down black rock beside the crossing. The bridge also provides an excellent view of the rich profusion of tree ferns growing in the creek bed below. Their brilliant green lacy crowns are one of the most exotic things I've ever seen.

I tell Dainis, "When we're back in those hot days at Lincoln, we'll think of this waterfall and the forest and say, 'Can we go back there?' "

He dips his helmeted head. "Yeah, we will."

BACK AT the house, Dainis and I are at loose ends as to what to do with the remainder of the day. Our speedy trap check took less than an hour and a half – we've obviously become more efficient. In the end, I write while he finishes preparing tracking tunnels for his Scout project, after which he reads, and lifts stamps from bits of envelope soaked in water.

JĀNIS AND VILIS HOME AFTER A LONG DAY IN THE FOREST

Five long hours after Dainis and I returned to the house, Vilis and Jānis ride the dripping, mud-spattered Yamaha into the yard. The quad is loaded with two empty stoat traps lashed to the roll bar behind Jānis, and red and green equipment tubs strapped to the front carrier. Beneath white motorcycle helmets, my husband's and son's faces are weary. When they enter the house and remove their outerwear, I see that their clothes are soaking wet from moisture that wicked its way beneath their raincoats and pants.

"Couldn't do it," Vilis tells me when I ask about the alternate route from Ten Man Hut. "There's a huge washout in the track. We couldn't get past it. That's why it took us so long. We had to drive all the way back."

Jānis enthuses about Ten Man Hut, telling me that it's built of corrugated metal and has a lean-to shelter, a stove, and a water barrel. Vilis adds that the hut is situated in a clearing atop a ridge and looks out over Tongariro Forest, beyond which, on a clear day, the volcanoes on the Central Volcanic Plateau are visible in the distance.

JĀNIS AT TEN MAN HUT

VIEW FROM TOP TRACK ON A CLEAR DAY

Again, the hot tub washes away Vilis's and the boys' chills. Then Vilis drives to National Park, a small town on the edge of Tongariro National Park. He stocks up on bread for us and petrol for the quads. He also washes and dries a load of clothes at the laundromat. No more hand-washing for me.

IN THE night, rain unlike any we've experienced in Ōwhango, drops like stones from the sky. The pounding deluge sweeps on and on. It declines in intensity then roars back in thunderous downpours. Vilis and I are repeatedly awakened by barrages on the metal roof above our heads. "I wonder what we'll see in the morning," he murmurs.

December 29

WHAKAPAPA RIVER is a boiling brown fury. It slams white-laced haystacks against the riverbanks and smashes, with deadly power, against rocks anchoring the bridge's supports. We stare at the torrent in awe and then watch in disbelief as river surfers launch sledges into the raging water.

Vilis decides that he alone will check and close stoat traps this morning, since other waterways will also be at peak flood levels. At the house, he loads stoat-processing gear onto the Yamaha, his face grim with the knowledge that some of the traps may have been inundated during the storm.

"Be careful," I urge.

He returns much earlier than expected. "The Little Mako is running so high, I thought the Yamaha's engine might stall if I attempted a crossing. I'll have to wait until later and hope the water level drops."

We drive to Taumarunui, where rain pours onto streets and Vilis discusses river crossings on quads with the proprietor of Honda First. The quad store owner assures him it's unlikely the Yamaha's engine would have stalled. On our return to Ōwhango, my husband again sets out to check the remaining traps.

The boys and I fill the ensuing nerve-wracking hours with house chores and a walk on Ōhinetonga Loop Track within the scenic reserve. Dainis is glum and lethargic, his feet dragging, as though the rain and his father's lengthy absence have robbed him of his usual good humour.

At 10:00 p.m., hours after the boys are tucked into their sleeping bags, Vilis returns in the darkness. He's drenched and looks utterly spent.

"Were you able to get to all the traps?" I ask, relief surging through me. He's safe.

"Yeah, but the tracks are in terrible condition. There are washouts everywhere."

I'm afraid to pose the next question. "Were there any stoats?"

He laughs without humour. "Three, if you can believe it. Sarah, and then Shiraz, who was dead, and then a new one. I called her Sally."

I stare at him. "But it's been so rare to catch any! It's ironic that they all were caught the night it stormed."

He tugs off his rain gear and sags into a chair. "Maybe they were looking for shelter."

December 30

DAINIS PEERS through the wall of windows behind the cushioned bench on which he rests in the living room. Tucked into his sleeping bag, he's feverish and drained after numerous trips to the bathroom.

No wonder his feet were dragging during our hike in the scenic reserve yesterday. Now he says morosely, "It's raining again."

"So, what should we do today?" Vilis asks, catching our attention.

"What's there *to* do?" Jānis inquires grouchily.

After seven straight days of rain, cabin fever has infected us with restlessness and bouts of ill humour.

"Let's brainstorm," Vilis suggests. "I'll write down all the possibilities, and then we'll go through them."

"What kind of possibilities?" Jānis asks, a hint of interest in his voice.

"Anything at all."

"Okay," Jānis says quickly, "Let's go mountain biking on the trails."

Vilis writes it down.

Other suggestions follow and are added to the list. Go cycling in Ōwhango. Stay home. Swim at Hidden Waterfall. Play cards. Drive Mud Track on quads. Go tramping somewhere.

"Play computer games all day," Dainis suggests slyly, knowing he and Jānis are usually limited to forty-five minutes a day.

Jānis grins his maverick grin. "Eat Dinky Toys with lots of ketchup."

The boys hoot with laughter when their father jots down these two possibilities.

"Go for a drive somewhere," Vilis suggests.

I shrug. "Do lots of baking."

"*Eat* lots of baking," Jānis says, laughing.

Vilis also writes these ideas down, and more, until the list spans the length of his paper. Next, we go through the list, and Vilis crosses off all the suggestions that are impossible (example: driving quads on Mud Track today, since we would get hopelessly stuck on the flooded track), and then crosses off all the items that fewer than two of us want to do (example: eating Dinky Toys with lots of ketchup). This process eliminates all the options except playing cards, driving somewhere, and eating lots of baking.

"How about a drive?" Vilis suggests.

"There's no point in going for a drive if you don't have somewhere to go," Jānis tells him. "And I don't want to."

Vilis dangles a worm. "We could have lunch in Taumarunui."

I add a couple more. "There's a red asterisk on the road map indicating a glow-worm cave at Kākahi. We could visit that on the way to Taumarunui. Plus, there's an old coal mine and conservation area west of Taumarunui. Maybe we could check them out, too."

Mollified, Jānis agrees, and Vilis and I cajole Dainis into agreeing to the outing.

We miss the first turn-off for Kākahi, but eventually find the village southeast of Taumarunui. The owner of the general store tells us the glow-worms can't be seen during the day and are not found in a cave. Rather, they're in a tunnel formed by vegetation that crowns a narrow road. As of yesterday, that road has a stretch under water and is washed out past the tunnel. "But you can drive through the water and park before the tunnel, if you want to have a look anyway," he assures us.

Cautiously, we follow his directions. As promised, the flooded section of road is easily crossed. We step inside the tunnel and are enchanted by its high, wet walls, green with ferns. A canopy of tree ferns and shrubs arches completely over the road for a distance of 200 metres, forming the tunnel's roof. "We'll definitely have to come back one night soon," I suggest. "A *dry* night."

In Taumarunui, we enjoy a Chinese food smorgasbord and

desserts from a bakery we discover while strolling the town's main street. Still feeling washed-out, Dainis doggy-bags much of his lunch and saves his apple turnover for later.

From Taumarunui, we drive west on a grey snake of highway that winds among endless green razorback ridges. Rain-swollen Whanganui River runs brown and wide at their bases. I gaze down plunging hillsides as Vilis steers the car along the serpentine road. It's even twistier than Summit Road in the Port Hills near Christchurch. "This road gets the ribbon for the twistiest in New Zealand," I mutter.

Dainis smiles. "What shape would the ribbon be, Magi?"

"Twisty. With lots of curls."

"Like ribbon candy," Vilis says. "The kind you get at Christmas."

LANDSCAPE WEST OF TAUMARUNUI

We follow the highway's tight curves along the top of a sharp ridge and turn onto a narrow gravel road, its edges crumbling into a murky, fast-flowing creek. The road ends at an embankment with a "BRIDGE CLOSED" sign posted beside it. Beyond the embankment, a weathered wooden bridge spans the creek. Its near edge is a straight grey line suspended in air and accessible only by a foot-wide column of soil. Shiny black coal flakes speckle the roadside cliff, but disappointingly, we can't find any mine.

With fleet and wary feet, we cross the eroding bridge and tramp the abandoned access road toward Waitānga Conservation Area. To the south, bladelike hills grazed into terraces and dotted with sheep stretch as far as the eye can see. Slimy sheep dung slides like grease under our shoes, and we spot wild turkeys – six in one flock plus a pair and a single bird – skulking through long grass outside sheep corrals. Vilis and the boys collect turkey feathers dropped on the old road, and Dainis spots a broken egg, large and white – likely a turkey egg, perhaps pillaged by a stoat, rat, or possum.

Rain returns, first as refreshing mist and later as insistent drizzle. We turn back and hurry down a long, curving slope toward the bridge, our destination marked by an immense pine tree that spreads like a giant fan coral against a backdrop of emerald hills softened by mist and the white fluffs of foraging sheep.

HIKING THROUGH SHEEP PASTURE WEST OF TAUMARUNUI

The drive home in pouring rain is quiet, and our evening

peaceful. Vilis and the boys play cards while I write. They play bridge, between the sheets, and lastly spoons, which is accompanied by loud, giddy laughter and mad scrambling for the two spoons, one of which ends up bent into a right angle. "Well," Jānis giggles, "Dainis said he wanted to play a more dignified game!"

December 31

Sʊʊʊʊʊʊʊ ʊʊʊʊʊ Vilis's helmet, while his bicycle is momentarily shrouded in mist rising from Whakapapa Bush Road. I also pass through the mist and feel the sun's warmth. Earlier this morning, the four of us gazed in dismay as sheets of water again plummeted from the sky and ricocheted off the Bomb. When the sun broke through at 9:30 a.m., we hastily clipped on helmets and jumped onto our bicycles.

We fly down the long hill toward Whakapapa River. Jānis zooms ahead, dodging eroded cracks that penetrate the road's pumice base like crooked, sunken fingers, a legacy of the deluge two days ago. I jounce over the shallowest cracks and skirt twenty-centimetre crevices that stretch halfway across the road.

"It feels so good to use my legs," Vilis calls back to me. "I've been sitting on quads and in cars too much lately."

"I know what you mean."

The river still runs high, but has dropped two metres. Beyond the bridge, Vilis and Jānis ride through narrow Deep Creek near the pumice quarry. Both yelp in surprise when their bikes bog down in the pebbly creek bed. Jānis loses his balance and steps into the shallow water. A second later, Vilis does the same.

"Yikes!" Jānis shouts.

"It's cold!" Vilis yells.

Dainis and I laugh as we take the bridge.

On quads, we pay no heed to the 42 Traverse's deceptively gentle upward grade kilometre after kilometre. Now, even with the bicycles in low gear, our legs push hard and our lungs strain. Jānis continues in the lead, his sturdy legs working overtime. Dainis brings up the rear, still somewhat drained from his sickness yesterday but game to continue. Three kilometres up the 42 Traverse and six kilometres from Ōwhango, Vilis notes Dainis's wan face and suggests we turn back.

Clouds sag onto the forest, spitting drizzle. Gravity pulls us down the long incline to the bridge, the effortlessness of our descent an ecstasy of speed. At the pumice quarry Dainis and I stop to don raincoats. The drizzle has changed to hard, slapping splashes. When I see he's ready, I pedal on, only to hear him call frantically, "Magi, stop! There's something wrong. My bike won't go." His front tire is flat.

Vilis and Jānis wait, crouched beneath protecting shrubs near the river. "It's too wet to patch the tire now," Vilis says. "We'll have to walk back."

"There's no point in all of us walking," I tell him. "Take Jānis home. He doesn't even have his raincoat."

My husband and younger son peddle across the bridge's smooth grey concrete and push hard on the hill to Ōwhango. Dainis and I walk home through the rain.

IN LATE afternoon, prepared with rain coats, rain pants, and rubber boots, we walk downhill from Ōwhango to Brock Farm to check out Ōwhango Black 2000, a shooting meet. *Boom!* A rifle's loud report fills the air, guiding our footsteps. A brief shower chases shooters from the range and urges us under sheltering trees until the competition resumes.

Colourful tents and two beige canvas teepees dot grassy fields adjacent to the pasturelike range. The field of shooters is sparse, and we're told that many contestants, discouraged by the wet weather, have already abandoned the week-long meet. We watch a middle-aged woman with a sleek cap of red hair fire a long-barrelled rifle. We're curious about the gun, which has a stock carved from golden brindled wood. Our curiosity sparks a deluge of information from a tall, ruddy-faced man standing near the woman. He tells us that the rifle is an American flintlock (a long rifle from the 1770s) and that its stock is curly maple. While the woman reloads, he provides a commentary on her actions.

We watch her pour a measured portion of black powder from a powder horn into the barrel. She places a small round cloth patch over the hole and a steel ball over the patch. She rams the ball and patch down into the upper part of the barrel with a short ramrod, then pushes them to the base of the barrel with a long ramrod. She's fast and efficient, her movements smooth with no sign of rushing. Finally, she pours a small amount of priming powder into the firing pan, a shallow, covered, metal hollow into which sparks from the flintlock hammer will shoot when the trigger is pulled. Those sparks will create a small explosion that will ignite the powder in the barrel and discharge the ball. The rifle has a double trigger. The rear one sets the hammer mechanism for firing. The front one is a hair trigger that releases the hammer with the lightest pressure. Now she's ready. We hold our hands over our ears. *Boom!* A puff of smoke billows from the barrel.

The rifles of the other contestants are even louder. Three enthusiastic Taumarunui men tell us their guns are replicas of caplock rifles used in North America in the eighteenth century. Instead of employing flint and a firing pan filled with priming powder to ignite the gunpowder in the barrel, the caplock rifles have a tiny firing cap that the hammer hits when released, causing a spark to shoot into the barrel. "Want to give it a try?" one of the men asks Vilis. My husband hastens to accept.

"How about you?" another asks me.

"How much does it hurt?" I inquire, having seen a man fire a massive blast from a prone position, then lie very still before nursing his shoulder.

The grizzled, bearded shooter laughs in response. "As much as you want it to. I can put in a light load for you."

"What's a light load?"

"Twenty or thirty grams."

"What's a regular load?"

He shrugs. "Most are shooting fifty."

"Sure. I'd like to try with a light load."

The targets are different from those at the rifle range in Tai Tapu, where Dainis and I shot along with the other Scouts and moms four months ago. Here, I aim at a bull's-eye, a single large black dot with concentric rings approaching it, rather than at eight small such dots. It seems a lifetime since I fired that .22 in Tai Tapu, yet when I raise this rifle, it feels familiar in my hands. I slide my left hand forward to balance the heavy barrel and place the bead sight over the centre of the target before releasing the hair trigger. *Boom!* The blast is muffled by my ear protectors, and with the light load, my shoulder barely feels the recoil. Nonetheless, I haven't a clue where the shot went.

The grizzled man, standing a few steps back, lifts his eyebrows when I turn to smile in thanks. "Not bad," he says. "Right between the nine and ten circles. Not bad at all for a first shot."

Dainis and Jānis also have a go with light loads. They're aided by a slight, wiry man who stands behind each in turn and helps them hold up the rifle and sight the target. It doesn't take Dainis long to fire his shot, but Jānis seems to stand forever. He looks small and fragile as he fights to balance the rifle. Then, *boom!* His shot is off and he's removing the ear protectors, his face a study of shyness and satisfaction.

The men are full of anecdotes. They tell of a fellow leaving his ramrod in his barrel during a timed competition, then rushing to grab it out before firing in record time. They inform us that one of the competitors here just returned from Australia, where he won a gold medal in the 600-metre event. They point out the black powder derivation of phrases such as "a flash in the pan," "going off half-cocked," and "keep your nose to the wind and your powder dry." They even explain that "cold enough to freeze the balls off a brass monkey" refers to a brass triangle that held cannon balls. The triangle contracted upon freezing, spilling the cannon balls. They would talk on, I'm sure, however we're standing in the middle of the long-distance range needed for the next event. Vilis, the boys, and I thank the men and walk up the unsealed road to Ōwhango, filled with warmth at the generous welcome we received.

LATER, MORE raindrops spatter the large windows at the house this New Year's Eve. Dainis, worn out from his stomach bug, is already asleep. Jānis, however, is glued to the computer, battling aliens and determined to stay up past midnight to greet the new year. Vilis and I read novels to keep him company.

Struck by a sudden thought, I look up from my book. "Vilis, on rifle targets…is the ten circle on the outside of the dot or in the centre?"

"In the centre," he tells me.

Ah. That explains the grizzled man's lifted eyebrows when I turned to thank him.

January 1, 2001

SUNSHINE GREETS the new year, and Vilis gives the go-ahead for all of us to resume fieldwork. With Jānis seated behind me, I turn the Honda quad into the flat pumice "parking lot" at the base of the quarry near Whakapapa River. Our morning task is to check the string of twenty tracking tunnels in the forest above the quarry. Vilis and Dainis roar past on the Yamaha to open traps that have remained closed since the violent rainstorm three days ago, during which one of three stoats seeking refuge in a trap, died.

Jānis and I check out the two tracks that lead to the top of the pumice quarry. They're even more deeply eroded than they were on Christmas Eve. On each track, a gaping crevice separates two parallel ribs of hard-packed pumice. Jānis points to the longer, steeper track. "Magi, come up this one. It's fun."

I shake my head. "I have a tracking tunnel on the other, so I'll go up it."

"Okay. Meet you at the top." As my son scampers up the tougher track, his feet dance from one pumice rib to the other and leap across the crevice as though daring it to claim him.

I hop from rib to rib on the shallower track. My shoulder bag, which is filled with track-collecting papers, peanut butter bait, and charcoal-paraffin oil mixture, bounces awkwardly against my hip with every step. Near the top of the track, I spot a bright orange flag. It cues me to the presence of a corrugated plastic tracking tunnel I would otherwise not have found in the dense shrubs beside the track. I collect rat prints and change the papers and bait in the tunnel, then reposition the tube in the thick vegetation.

"There you are." Arms crossed, Jānis waits for me where the two tracks merge at the top of the quarry and lead into Tongariro Forest. We enter its dark, shaded beauty, where he exclaims over the muddiness of the track and the depth of water-filled mudholes. Leaves drip moisture, and fallen tree fern fronds resemble orange-brown pennants scattered over the forest floor. Hidden Waterfall sings louder, with rich white choruses tumbling down its rocky throat. The narrow creek at its feet today rumbles in light harmony.

We stride over the tree fern bridge, its spongy black trunks now nearly submerged, and check tunnel after tunnel. A few of the sodden papers, no doubt drenched during the recent deluge, are almost worn away, and one is spattered with mud from a passing quad. A good number are decorated with rat prints, but none with stoat prints. I crouch and replace papers in a tunnel beside the track, then straighten at the sound of a motor.

A greenish boat-like vehicle ploughs toward us, its six wheels churning up mud. The all-terrain vehicle is driven by a middle-aged man accompanied by two smiling, teenaged girls.

Jānis and I move out of the way.

The vehicle passes, then stops. "We've seen your flags and those boxes all along the track. What are they?" the man asks.

"They're tracking tunnels." I hold up the tunnel I just checked. "We're hoping to find areas with stoats, so we set out tunnels like this to collect small mammal tracks. An animal enters the tunnel and has to walk across the oily charcoal to get to the bait." I angle the tunnel so that all three can see into it. "Then it leaves its footprints on the paper on its way out."

"Found any stoats?" the man asks.

"Not yet on this track. Just rats."

"Work for DOC?"

"No. For Landcare, in association with DOC."

He nods. "We have a weekend house in Ōwhango. We always come up for a couple of weeks during the holidays." He gestures to one of the girls. "My daughter's friend from Dunedin is visiting, so I thought we'd show her some of the trails."

"Absolutely." I smile at the two girls. "Enjoying your break from school?"

"Yeah." They smile back, nodding vigorously.

"Well, we'll leave you to it," the man says cheerfully, setting the all-terrain vehicle into motion.

"That was one of those ATVs that floats," Jānis comments.

"They'll need it on this track."

"Oh, yeah! There's that *big* hole you can't drive around. And that *really* deep one. They'll be able to go right through them."

We approach the cliff-top lookout carefully, wary because there may be new erosion on the already sheer rock face above Whakapapa River. The lookout shelter is as it was, however, so we slip inside for a brief view of the scene below. Rushing river. Green pastures. Cream-and-green building, with tents and two tepees pitched nearby. "That *is* the farm where the black powder shoot is!" Jānis exclaims, confirming the possibility the four of us discussed yesterday, that what we'd initially thought from the lookout was a farmhouse is actually the gun club's meeting house.

Jānis and I slip out of the lookout shelter and search for the remaining tunnels. Sunshine washes us with welcome warmth in grassy clearings and abandons us in shady forest, where damp air is spiced with scents of bark and fern. After dealing with the last tunnel, we head for the pumice quarry and chuckle when we see the all-terrain vehicle's fresh, wide-spaced tracks leading straight into and out of each mudhole, even the massive ones. They also mark the ribs of the steepest pumice track.

"Let's go!" Jānis challenges me, his eyes alight.

We romp down the track, leaping from rib to rib in a daring dance, the eroded crevice a gaping gash beneath our feet.

When Vilis and Dainis return from opening stoat traps, Dainis nearly vibrates with excitement. "You should see the tracks, Magi! They're really bad. You for sure won't like them now. There are washouts everywhere."

"And lots of precarious crossings," Vilis adds.

Dainis laughs. "There was even a jeep that had fallen off the track onto its side."

"A *jeep*? What was a jeep doing in there anyway?" I ask.

"Who knows?" Vilis shrugs. "Trying to drive across."

"Were you able to get to all the traps?" I ask him.

"Yeah. The crossings had been repaired enough to get across, with tree ferns and boards and whatever."

Dainis grins. "We boiled up some water beside the track and made hot chocolate." He nods with satisfaction. "It was fun."

In mid-afternoon, Dainis begins his tracking tunnel research project in Ōhinetonga Scenic Reserve. He inspects vegetation beside the loop track near Whakapapa River Bridge. Here, blackberry canes and shrubs form a virtually impenetrable wall of scrub on both sides of a dirt track that meanders through a narrow belt of grasses and wildflowers. "I'll put the first one here," he decides. He labels a length of flagging tape "D1" and attaches it to a shrub.

Behind Dainis, Vilis carries twenty of the forty tracking tunnels Dainis assembled, fifteen in a big brown backpack, and five in his hands. He paces off five metres along the trail past the flag and hands Dainis a tunnel also labelled D1. Dainis kneels in the grass and removes two bait containers from a canvas bag slung over his shoulder. He baits the oil-charcoal panel in the centre of the tunnel floor with a dab of peanut butter and a large bead of mince (ground beef). After rising to his feet, he positions the tunnel amid dense grasses at the base of a shrub a couple metres back from the trail. He applies gentle, side-to-side pressure to test the tunnel's stability on the ground surface, then nods.

SETTING TRACKING TUNNELS IN SCRUB HABITAT

Vilis paces off thirty metres, and Dainis attaches a new flag, D2, to a branch. He repeats the baiting and setting procedure for another tunnel, the second of ten he'll set in the first habitat, riverside scrub. After those are in position, he'll set ten more tunnels in a second habitat, forest with thick understory, farther along the track.

I stroll and bird while Vilis and Jānis assist Dainis with his tracking tunnels. It's an idyllic afternoon. Dragonflies cruise near the river. A huge bumblebee and smaller honeybees delve for nectar in blackberry blossoms. Fantails flirt with me, spreading wide their showy white-bordered, black-centred tails. A saffron-suffused, sparrowlike yellowhammer zooms along the trail. Blackish-brown *tūī* wing between trees, their paired balls of white feathers (*poi*) dangling like pendants from their dark necks.

TŪĪ FEEDING ON NEW ZEALAND FLAX NECTAR

I climb a portion of track that clings to a cliffside high above Whakapapa River and offers unimpeded views of the waterway. The air is ripped by a rough shriek, and I spot my first long-tailed cuckoo flying across the river. Its plumage is all barred and streaked brown, its wings sharp angles, its long tail trailing. This bird is one of New Zealand's two native cuckoo species. The second is the shining cuckoo, which I heard singing its up/down sliding notes while Vilis showed off the young male stoat, Sarah, to our sons during our first day of fieldwork. Like other cuckoos, the long-tailed cuckoo is a nest parasite.

I chat with two elderly couples tramping the track, and then leisurely retrace my steps down the cliffside trail. By the time Dainis has set his last tunnel, afternoon has turned to evening. "I am *so* hungry," he groans. We hurry back along a trail now decorated with bright orange flags, with only one thought on our minds. *Food*.

January 2

THE FOREST soars above Dainis and me. Slim and massive trunks raise branches up into the light thirty metres or more above our heads, thirty metres or more above the shaded forest floor, empty of vegetation except for widespread ferns and tree ferns. It's as though we're not *in* the forest, but beneath it.

This morning, I'm the gofer carrying folded tracking tunnels and pacing out distances for Dainis, who is setting tunnels in the third of his four chosen habitats, mature open forest. We have the track to ourselves, and our footsteps fall silently on damp, humus-rich soil. Peace surrounds us.

I tell Dainis, "When we get home to Nova Scotia, I think I'll want to let more of our land grow into forest and just leave it as forest."

He looks at me in surprise. "Why?"

"Because there's so little forest left there. There's so much logging. And what forests there are, are so managed. I don't want to manage our forest, except to maybe cut a log or two when we need them. I just want it to be." I grin at him. "I need to become a rich writer so I can buy up all the land around our place and let it grow into forest."

He grins, too. We both know the likelihood of that happening.

AN HOUR later, we scramble up and down a steep, thinly wooded slope bordering Ōhinetonga Lagoon. Sharp-edged palm ferns slap our faces and scratch our hands as we thrash through clumps taller than my head. Rain bounces off leaves and dents the surface of the narrow water body, but Dainis and I don't feel it. This is habitat number four, lagoon edge, and it's a whole different ballgame from the open forest that was number three. That was easy; this is demanding. That was serene; this is exciting. We slip on greasy climbs and squelch across water-logged ground, discovering a lovely three-metre waterfall and a shared sense of adventure. I'm becoming intrigued by the mystery of what tracks Dainis will find in his four chosen habitats.

ŌHINETONGA LAGOON

AFTER LUNCH, I prowl through the house, knowing I should write more entries in my journal but wanting desperately to go somewhere new, to see sites as yet unseen. The weather is "anything could happen" cloud and clear, but it's the first weekday afternoon that we're all home at the same time with no stoat work scheduled. So, I propose an outing, a walk, somewhere.

"Where?" Vilis asks in surprise. "I thought you wanted time to write in your journal."

"I know, but we've had so few chances to get out and do things here. I thought we would have more opportunities for day and afternoon trips away from Ōwhango. And the weather's been so rotten."

The boys groan. After spending the morning in the field, they're not interested in hiking.

"Let's drive to Whakapapa," Vilis finally suggests. "There's a visitor information centre there that I'm sure can tell us about walks in the area. Then I can check at DOC for that missing research box, too. We can even throw in some laundry at the laundromat on our way home."

Decision made, we cram rain gear, coats and hats, water bottles, apples, and trail mix into our day packs and drive twenty-five minutes to Whakapapa, a park and ski field village at the base of the active volcano Ruapehu. Whakapapa houses the headquarters of Tongariro National Park and provides lodging for skiers bound for Whakapapa Ski Field. As we near the village, my eyes drink in the sight of the trio of volcanoes rising high above grassland and forest on the Central Volcanic Plateau.

Vilis points. "Look at the snow on Ruapehu!"

Glistening snow so white it hurts my eyes tops the massive volcanic peak. Long fingers of white reach far lower on the mountain's slopes than when we last saw it on our drive to and from Lake Taupō before Christmas. The highest mountain on North Island, Ruapehu reaches 2 797 metres and bears eighteen glaciers, the only ones on North Island.[31] A crater lake atop the peak periodically heats up due to its proximity to magma within the cone. The water's warming cycles may coincide with eruptions of steam and ash.[32]

"Even Ngāuruhoe has snow." I nod to the tall, slender cone north of Ruapehu. Streaks of white run down its upper slopes. A thick halo of grey-blue cloud obscures its summit.

"It looks like it's erupting now, and that's the ash cloud," Vilis says.

"Does Tongariro have snow?" Jānis asks from the back seat.

"No, not that I can see," I reply.

Long before we enter Whakapapa, we see the Grand Chateau (now Chateau Tongariro) with its blue roof, red brick upper floors, and yellow lower floors looming up from the tawny vegetation that cloaks the lower mountain slopes. The village itself is small and clean, its main street lined with vehicles near the visitor centre, its sidewalks busy with the foot traffic of tourists.

We drive to the Department of Conservation compound adjacent to park headquarters, where Vilis finds the Kiwi Room open and news that the long-awaited research box has arrived. Next door, the visitor centre for Tongariro National Park offers so much more than we have time for, including displays and videos about volcanoes and the park's creation. As we study track descriptions, I decide that the boys and I will return next week and study it all as a special homeschool project. Today, we only have time for walking, and we opt for Taranaki Falls Track, a two-hour loop that features a twenty-metre waterfall.

A cold wind blows off the volcanoes, so we bundle up as we start the track, only to remove coats when the path enters the shelter of a beech forest edging rocky Wairere Stream. The boys are weary and uninterested until we exit the forest and scramble up onto a moor. Here, introduced heath plants have encroached on native grassland growing on ash soils formed as a result of past volcanic eruptions. According to an interpretive sign, the ash was deposited in a circular pattern surrounding the three volcanoes and created the Ring Plain on which we walk. Jānis finds the bleached skeleton of a rabbit or hare, identifiable as a lagomorph (rabbit family) by its powerful hind legs and the tiny, peg-like teeth behind its central incisors. He also discovers that the low, thick vegetation is perfect for playing "hide and sneak." He ducks down out of sight behind a dense shrub and crawls toward Vilis and me.

"Oh, I see your hat!" Vilis shouts.

Jānis springs up, then grins and hides again. Dainis joins in the game, and soon both boys are bounding through the moor, diving into cover, and sneaking toward Vilis and me.

When the kids tire of the game, we return to the track and follow it beside the stream's rocky gorge and through uplands where stunted plants grow in scattered clumps on barren, stony soil.

WAIRERE STREAM AND VOLCANIC UPLANDS

The focus of the track, Taranaki Falls, is like a wedding dress. Its white-water bodice froths through a narrow channel carved in black rock and fans into a wide, lacy skirt that pounds onto rocks below.

Beyond the falls, we tramp across upland moors on slopes that rise in the distance to the bulk of Ruapehu. Vilis tosses out a question, "What do you miss most while living in New Zealand?"

"Food or what?" Jānis asks.

"Anything."

"I miss my gardens and all the fresh fruits and vegetables," I reply.

Dainis says, "I miss my LEGO."

"I miss snow," Vilis tells us.

Jānis considers, then says, "The food I miss most from Canada is Kraft Dinner."

"Really?" Vilis laughs. "And we're not even somewhere with weird food. What other foods do you miss?"

"Cheerios," Dainis replies, referring to the toasted oat cereal that we enjoy for breakfasts in Nova Scotia.

"Hot dogs," chips in Jānis.

"Real donuts," Dainis adds.

"I think," Jānis plans cheerfully, "that the first day we're at our house in Nova Scotia, we'll have Cheerios for breakfast, Kraft Dinner for lunch, hot dogs for supper, and donuts for dessert."

Later, back at the house in Ōwhango, Vilis notices that the small radio receiver he uses to tune in transmitter signals from the radio-collared stoats is missing. Frustrated, he tries to figure out where he could have left it after checking the stoat traps this morning. I leave him to his pondering. As I climb the stairs to our bedroom, I glance out a window and see stars lighting the night sky. With a start of surprise, I realize Orion is upside down.

January 3

I'M WRITING, and the boys are still in their sleeping bags when Vilis returns from closing the stoat traps and searching for the missing radio receiver.

"Did you find it?" I ask.

"Yep."

"At the trap?"

"Yep."

"Good. Does it still work?"

"I haven't tested it yet." He slides the glass patio door closed. "*Brrr!* It's cold out there. I had on my sweatpants and sweatshirt, sweater, coat, rain gear, and gloves, and I was *still* cold. And this is summer on the North Island!"

"In the subtropical forest," I add teasingly.

"Yeah!"

He shivers and grabs a coffee before loading the Honda quad I've been driving onto a trailer behind the station wagon. It's due back at Landcare in Palmerston North, a three-hour drive south from Ōwhango. As he straps the quad to the trailer, our next-door neighbour, an elderly man, calls over the fence, "How's the trapping going?"

Thus begins a forty-minute conversation during which Vilis and I learn that the neighbour, Ted, drove logging trucks along what are now quad tracks in Tongariro Forest, and that he worked with Frank Climo, after whom the one-way-only Climo's Track (down, that is; never up) is named. Ted gives us a few pointers on fishing spots, and he and Vilis compare notes on the state of deterioration of the tracks.

A few minutes later, Vilis takes his leave and I walk into a lit powder keg in the house. The boys are at odds over who has reading dibs on the *Harry Potter* book, and who can use the computer. Jānis, who is exhausted after staying up late last night, is grouchy and belligerent, angry and wounded. He flares out at Dainis, who is cool and aloof, aggravating his younger brother even more by ignoring his questions and remaining icily polite. I become the mediator, struggling for fairness and to bolster sagging self-esteem.

Later, the boys and I slam and miss balls on one of the rough old tennis courts Tala showed us two weeks ago. Our swinging, dashing figures are miniscule compared with the rainforest giants that tower above us, draping lush branches over the fence like amused spectators. Our play is poor, with hard feelings carried onto the court from my sons' earlier disagreements and snide comments to each other. Here in Ōwhango, sibling rivalry rears an even bigger head than in Lincoln. It's exacerbated by the amount of time the boys spend in each other's company, the wet weather, the lack of activities outside of research, Jānis's desire to do everything his big brother can do, and Dainis's expertise at pushing exactly the right buttons to aggravate Jānis.

I make a wild slam. The ball *thunks* into a tree trunk and bounces back onto the court. Jānis wallops it over the fence into the forest. The three of us creep through tangles of vines and shrubs and around thick trees to find it, paying for our success with drops of blood given to blackberry thorns and the backward-pointing barbs of bush lawyer, a trailing forest plant that snags our skin and clothes. After we find the ball, we sweat away our tensions with more tennis. As we play, the notes of a bellbird's liquid song drop like glistening pearls of peace onto the forest.

We take some of that peace with us when we return to the house. Their tempers soothed, the boys build houses of cards on the living room carpet. They construct intricate circles, squares, and lines of houses, with roofs balanced on upright cards.

And on the counter, a piece of white paper dries after Jānis stamped it with handmade potato stamps dipped in paint. In the paper's centre, a bright green oval contains the rough image of a tree fern. It's surrounded by four royal blue ovals, each containing the image of a kiwi. I notice a distinct progression in the clarity of the kiwi images in a clockwise fashion around the tree fern, although Jānis didn't stamp them in a clockwise pattern. It's as though out of randomness has come unintended order; as though in this simple piece of art, the whole is suddenly and stunningly greater than the sum of its parts. *Rise of the Kiwi*. I'm struck by the way in which beauty can arise out of play, and by how easily I get caught up in what needs to be done and forget the joys of spontaneous creativity.

AT 8:00 P.M., Vilis drives into the yard. The boys and I rush to greet him.

"Have you eaten?" I ask.

"Junk food."

"Come in. I'll warm supper for you."

"*Eee-ew!*" Dainis grimaces. "He's got chips in a bag with mice right beside them.

"*Mice?*" Vilis and I ask in confusion.

Dainis looks again. "Oh, those aren't mice. They're donuts. The white kind with icing sugar on them."

White mice. White donuts. Stoat bait has made a *big* impression on this boy.

January 4

DAINIS BACKS the Yamaha quad out of its parking spot, only to come to an abrupt halt. He looks down and realizes the quad is still chained to Tala's work Honda, a security measure. "Oops!" An embarrassed grin spreads across his face.

Vilis unlocks the chain, and moments later he and Dainis roar out of the yard, with Dainis grinning and waving. They'll set traps along the far reaches of the 42 Traverse and on Top Track. With only one work quad at our disposal now, both the amount of territory Vilis can cover for his research and the boys' quad-riding time have been halved.

"Let's go biking. Explore Ōwhango," I suggest to Jānis, having noted the despondent look on his face. We cycle across the nearby railway track and highway and leisurely check out the village's few streets. Our exploration ends at the domain, where a surprise awaits us. Lush green playing fields have been transformed into a show ring. Trim young riders wearing white jodhpurs, dark jackets, and helmets ride horses with gleaming satin coats and braided manes. This horse show is as unexpected as the hidden tennis courts.

After watching several contestants ride, we cycle back to the house and listen for Vilis's and Dainis's return. Jānis builds card houses and draws pictures of New Zealand birds. While I putter, it occurs to me that Ōwhango is the only place I've lived where the sound of quads is more noticeable than that of cars. Here, train and quad choruses blend in a collage of far and near.

I grow uneasy as the time passes 4:00 p.m., by which hour Vilis was sure he and Dainis would return. With dry weather in the forecast, we'd planned a campout for tonight in one of the clearings alongside Mariner's Track. *Will we still have time to quad there and set up camp before dark?*

An hour later, the Yamaha finally roars up the driveway, and Vilis tells me the flood-damaged tracks slowed their work. Minutes later, the four of us pack camping gear and food onto the Yamaha and Tala's work Honda. Then we head out.

Whakapapa Bush Road is the driest I've seen it. Dust billows from beneath the Yamaha's tires, and I drop back to avoid it. This is the first time I've driven a quad since the deluge six days ago, and I quickly realize that Tala's quad pulls to the right. On the 42 Traverse, I see where the jeep fell into the washout, and gingerly direct the Honda over a bumpy, sand-bagged bridge bordered by two eroded holes. The tracks really *are* in terrible condition, with lots of precarious crossings. The Honda is sluggish on uphill runs due to the heavy pack behind Dainis. "I'm glad we're not going up the Big Mako like this," he yells to me. "We'd tip."

On Mariner's Track, I drive by feel, unable to see the track through the dense *mānuka* and sunlit *toetoe* crowding it. After scraping through shrubs beside a huge, mucky hole, Dainis and I meet Vilis and Jānis in the chosen grassy clearing peppered with cabbage trees. Nearby, a creek flows through a deep, tree-lined ravine. Vilis runs his gaze over the clearing. "Now *this* is what camping should be like!" he says happily. "Not with people all around. Isn't this a beautiful spot?"

Dainis grins. "And the quads are our steeds."

We set up camp after scouting for a tent site with as few hummocks as possible. Then, giddily enthralled with being in a tent, as usual, the boys throw sleeping bags at each other and wrestle, as though within those four slanted walls they've found the best of playgrounds. When we brush our teeth after a late supper of chilli, moon shadows paint sharply delineated shapes on silvery grasses. Vilis hangs a single candle lantern inside the tent. The vegetation surrounding us is too dry to hang any outdoors. While he reads from *Home is a Tent*, in which author Myrtle Simpson and her husband Hugh are now in Surinam, moonlight shines through our tent window and I hear a distinctive bird call I've not heard before.

"Listen! There's a morepork."

Frozen into silence, we distinguish the clear "*more-pork*" call of New Zealand's only native owl. Jānis gives me a thumbs-up, and I decide I'll rise at dawn for some early birding.

January 5

MY PLANS for dawn birding have gone awry. I thought I hadn't slept at all because of an annoying hummock, but in reality I slept too long! At 7:40 a.m., the sun is bright. Dew drenches the clearing's grasses. Clumps of *toetoe* hang pale seed flags. Cabbage trees thrust spiky balls of leaves against blue sky and the dark green face of Tongariro Forest.

TOETOE AND CABBAGE TREES EDGING OUR CAMP CLEARING

To battle the morning's damp cold, we crouch close to our portable camp stove and eat a hot porridge breakfast, plus eggs that

Dainis fries. Then we break camp quickly, since we all have fieldwork to do. Vilis and Jānis will check tracking tunnels and close stoat traps for the weekend. Dainis and I will collect and move his tracking tunnels to new sites in the riverside scrub and dense forest habitats. Vilis allows the boys to turn the quads around. Then we again face the jabbing, slicing gauntlet of Mariner's Track. Mud splashes onto our clothes, and *toetoe* seeds stick to my pile vest.

Back at the house, we drop our camping gear in a messy pile we'll clean up later, and gather field equipment. Knowing we'll be gone for hours, we eat a snack, then leave the house at 10:00 a.m. Vilis and Jānis roar off on the Yamaha. Dainis and I take the car, and I park near Whakapapa River Bridge.

In the late morning heat, my older son and I collect the orange flags and tracking tunnels he placed in riverside scrub four days ago. We find the first four tunnels quickly, but the D5 flag eludes us, as though it's been ripped from its attachment and stolen away. Again and again, I pace the distance back from D6 to where the flag and tunnel should be, but we can't find them. "Let's leave the D6 flag and move on," I say. "We can search for D5 again later."

We find the remaining five tunnels without incident, and of the nine collected, five have rat or mice tracks, and some have both. Dainis replaces the papers and charcoal-oil medium where necessary and sets six of the tunnels in a new stretch of scrub. Then he runs out of habitat.

"There's more scrub near the bridge," I tell him.

"But I want to look for D5 first," he insists.

We do, and again fail to find it. We repeat the procedure a half dozen times. I pace the distance from D6; Dainis scans the forest. Still, no success.

Again, we abandon the hunt temporarily, this time to collect the ten tunnels Dainis set in nearby dense forest, two of which contain rat tracks. Then we slog up a steep, mucky trail to a drier section of Ōhinetonga Loop Track. Dainis sets the ten tunnels at new sites within dense forest. All the while, the nagging mystery of the missing D5 hangs over us. After finishing with the forest tunnels, Dainis sets three more tunnels in patches of blackberry and shrubs near the river.

Hours have flown by. It's late afternoon, and hunger gnaws at our bellies. We expected to return to the house in time for a late midday meal, so didn't bring any food with us. Nonetheless, in one last bid to find D5, we again hurry to D6 and I pace back to where the missing flag should be, but is not. We're sweaty and hot and tired, but I repeat the procedure again and again. Then, as I scan the thick vegetation alongside the track for a glimpse of bright orange, I spot it. The flag is disguised by dead tree fern fronds and almost hidden behind a tree fern trunk.

"There it is!" I shout.

Dainis jerks toward it in near disbelief. I pace off five metres, and he spots and retrieves the tunnel, which has tracks. He resets it at the edge of a scrubby track leading into a marshy area near the river. Then we rush back to the car, amazed that this task, which we thought we would complete in two or three hours, required *seven* hours instead.

On our return to the house, Vilis exclaims, "Finally! We wondered what was taking you so long."

Dainis explains about D5, laughing now that the ordeal of finding the missing flag is over.

Jānis excitedly reports, "We caught a new stoat! A female."

"Really! Where?" I ask.

"Along Top Track," Vilis replies.

THIS DARK SHELTERING FOREST 111

"What's her name?" Dainis asks.

"Sarah II," Jānis answers. "That was Vilis's choice."

JĀNIS AND SARAH II

"Jānis was my assistant," Vilis says. "He handed me pliers and other tools and took pictures."

Our younger son's eyes shine. "And I got to pet Sarah II when she was tranquilized. Her fur was really soft."

After three weeks of trapping, the number of radio-collared stoats again stands at three. That sample size is too small to determine how far juvenile stoats disperse, particularly when only one, the male Sarah, is a juvenile. It appears less likely that Vilis will be able to complete his research project.

After our meal, I shower away dried sweat and dirt. Rarely has a hot wash felt so good. Then I slide a sundress over my head and relax in the living room with a thick book, the perfect ending to an intense and memorable research day

.January 6

MIST HANGS in the early morning air. It shrouds the forest and yard with secrets. I lose myself in writing while Dainis, accompanied by Vilis and Jānis, collects the first set of tracking tunnels from the open forest habitat and resets them at a new site within Ōhinetonga Scenic Reserve.

"Nothing," Dainis calls to me when they return after a quick hour and a half. "Just some *wētā* and other insects."

"Zero tracks," Vilis confirms. "That tells me that if there aren't any rats and mice in those forests, there aren't any stoats either."

Interesting. Data so far: 60 percent of Dainis's tracking tunnels in riverside scrub had small mammal tracks, 20 percent of his tunnels in the forest with thick understory had tracks, and 0 percent of the tracking tunnels in the open forest had tracks. *What about the lagoon-edge habitat?*

We postpone collecting the lagoon-edge tunnels until afternoon, as we need to buy supplies from Taumarunui. We drive to the Heart of the King Country and stock up on groceries and petrol for the quads. After shopping, Dainis and I savour long apple turnovers heavy with chunky apple filling while Vilis and Jānis devour chocolate-iced donuts bursting with real whipped cream. "That bakery is the best-kept secret in Taumarunui," I say, licking my fingertips.

Today, the central North Island town isn't bouncing with heat waves or awash with pouring rain. We complete our list of errands as effortlessly as orange and black goldfish swim through weeds in the fishpond beside the town's main street.

DURING THE afternoon, dragonflies and red-bodied damselflies skim above Ōhinetonga Lagoon, the latter mating in the air. Fantails and *tūī* flit around in shrubs near the lagoon edge, and wary ducks lift from the water. Human voices echo, bouncing back and forth across the narrow water body while Dainis, Jānis, and Vilis fight their way through scraping, swiping fern fronds to retrieve the ten tunnels Dainis and I set in the lagoon-edge habitat four days ago. "Ninety percent rat tracks, zero percent mice tracks," Dainis shouts to me before re-setting the tunnels farther around the lagoon.

I'm birding in open forest atop the steep slope beside the lagoon. Here, tree ferns rise to ten metres, their green circular sprays of fronds tracing mandalas against the sky. On the forest floor, infant tree ferns are thick, curled fiddleheads a foot tall, hirsute with bristling rusty hairs. Although massive, they remind me of the ostrich fern fiddleheads my family gathers from river floodplains in Nova Scotia each May, to eat as spring greens.

I amble among the tree ferns and widely spaced, towering

tawa trees. The *tawa's* narrow, lanceolate leaves form a lacy canopy high above me. In the treetops, noisy whiteheads – small native songbirds with white heads and underparts – trill and chatter while moving rapidly within the leafy canopy. Otherwise, the forest is still and serene, an ocean of peace, sheltered within the grandeur of its rising giants.

More than any other of my interests, this simple kind of on-foot exploration of the natural world is what moves me, what thrills and soothes me. I feel grounded. In harmony. Connected with a thousand organisms in Creation even though I'm alone. I stare at a tree fern, and my mind seeks words to describe it. I hear the whiteheads, and sentences begin. Two and a half decades ago, after spending seven years studying biology at university, I realized that when I go for a walk in the outdoors, I'm not thinking about experiments and hypotheses. I'm thinking about words. Words to describe what I see and hear and smell and feel around me, like this rainforest.

I stroll parallel to the lagoon edge, then abandon the forest and scramble downhill to join my husband and sons at the water's northern limit. Here, tall clumps of palm fern give way to dense blackberry canes, vines, and *toetoe* next to Whakapapa Bush Road. We aim for the road and thrash our way through ten metres of scrub. Thorns tear at our skin, *toetoe* leaves slap and slice us, and vines entangle our legs.

"Ow!" I yelp.

"Yikes!" Dainis shouts.

"Yeesh!" Jānis yells.

Finally we stumble out onto the road and climb into the Bomb, the boys laughing about the tough scrub. Back at the house, I brush *toetoe* seeds from my hair, wipe away blood from blackberry scratches, and then start supper.

"Why don't we go see the glow-worms tonight?" I suggest during the meal. "It's not raining. In fact, it's a beautiful night."

"That sounds like a good idea," Vilis says.

In the quiet beauty of a calm, moonlit evening, we return to the glow-worm tunnel at Kākahi and step into its darkness. Almost instantly, we see constellations of miniature blue stars against the blackness. The glow-worms (called *titiwai* in Māori, meaning "lights reflected on water")[33] are everywhere. On the dirt walls. In the ferns beside us. In the vegetation above us.

"Look in this hole!" Dainis calls.

We peer into a blue-lit recess in the tunnel wall and observe tiny, wormlike creatures. These are the carnivorous larvae of a gnat, *Arachnocampa luminosa*. The blue bioluminescence they produce, though enthralling to us, heralds a death trap for other insects. "They use the light to attract prey," I tell the boys, and we notice that the glow-worms lie amid transparent strands that resemble spider web silk. I've read that adult gnats also produce the blue light, although they use it to attract a mate rather than a meal.[34]

We discover more glow-worms in the vegetation and walls beside us and revel in the sheer beauty of those so high above us that all we can see is their light. At the tunnel's end, we step out into moonlight, the night sky far brighter than the tunnel's blackness. Then we re-enter the glow-worm tunnel and again revel in its blue beauty.

January 7

VILIS DRAGS three long slabs of densely celled foam insulation from under the house. "These will work."

Dainis and Jānis whoop with excitement. With the stoat traps closed for the weekend, we're looking for something fun to do this afternoon.

We don swimsuits, pile into the car, and drive Whakapapa Bush Road through Ōhinetonga Scenic Reserve until we're opposite the spot where Ōhinetonga Loop Track crosses the gravel road. Vilis parks the car at the roadside, and the boys and I carry the foam slabs as we follow the track through the old growth forest, with its towering *tawa*, to Ōhinetonga Lagoon.

We walk onto the boardwalk that spans the lagoon, and while Vilis plunges into the brown-tinted water, my sons and I lay the buoyant foam slabs on the lagoon's surface and scramble onto them. We paddle with our arms and feet to propel the slabs away from the boardwalk.

"The water's cold!" I yelp.

"It's *fresh*," Vilis calls out, his wet hair plastered to his skull.

"This is fun!" Dainis strikes out for the lagoon's centre, and Jānis follows him. Their laughter and chatter echo off the steep slope bordering the water.

The lagoon's calm surface is a skating rink for orange-red damselflies, and the air above it, a war zone for dragonflies defending territories. Pairs of damselflies mate in the air around us, their abdomens tightly curled and their bodies flying in tandem. They're blue, brown-green, or orange-red.

Reflections of tall shoreline trees and clumps of ferns and reeds spill over the lagoon surface, creating muted shades of olive green spattered with small orange and blue highlights that are the vivid damselflies. Near shore, a single white water lily is a globe of purity on a lily pad. Fantails perform acrobatics in trees near the water's edge, their reflected images dancing on the water surface.

"I'm surprised how few birds there are in this edge habitat," I call to Vilis.

"I'm surprised there's nobody else swimming in this lagoon," he responds.

Stay away! This is perfection.

We've discovered a Tongariro treasure.

January 8

AT THE Tongariro National Park Visitor Centre in Whakapapa, my sons and I learn that volcanic blocks are solid pieces of magma ejected during a volcanic eruption, whereas volcanic bombs are liquid magma ejections. We compare the sizes of dust clouds from past volcanic eruptions, which are symbolized by diagrams on a wall. Ruapehu's cloud is small, about the size of a Canadian quarter or New Zealand dollar coin. Tongariro's is larger, about the same as that of Vesuvius, which erupted in 79 A.D. and buried Pompeii. The Krakatoa eruption of 1883 is represented by a balloon-size cloud, and that of the Taupō caldera eruption in 189 A.D. by a cloud a metre in diameter. And then, as though these eruptions that shook the earth, buried landscapes and towns, and blackened the skies with dust and ash were nothing, we see the dust cloud of the Ōruanui eruption 26 500 years ago. It rises in a grey mass that would be taller than the ceiling if the ceiling hadn't stopped it. My imagination staggers. This country truly rests on the fiery guts of the earth.

We explore more of the visitor centre, entering a small theatre just in time to view a video called *The Gift of Tongariro*. The film informs us that Tongariro National Park was the first national park created in New Zealand and the fourth in the world. It was also the first parkland in the world to be bequeathed to the public by indigenous peoples. Concerned that farming, forestry, and rival tribes' land claims would endanger the integrity and prestige (*mana*) of the mountaintops sacred to his people, Te Heuheu Tūkino IV, high chief of the Ngāti Tūwharetoa tribe, made a sacred gift of Tongariro, Ngāuruhoe, and Ruapehu to all the people of New Zealand on September 23, 1887. From his initial gift, the park grew into the 79 598-hectare UNESCO Cultural and Natural World Heritage Site it is today.[35]

Historian Keith Sinclair wrote that for the Māori, their land was "life itself and more. It is impossible to exaggerate their love for their tribal lands, scene of a thousand ancestral deeds or ancient legends which were recounted endlessly and in loving detail…"[36] When we exit the interpretive centre, I see a quote from Te Heuheu Tūkino IV carved into a rock. It states, "The breath of my mountain is my heart." In those words, I catch a glimpse of the Māori's deep attachment to their ancestral lands.

Outside the centre, the boys and I follow a nature walk that illustrates vegetation zones in the park: forest, shrubland, grassland, and low-growing alpine plant associations. An information panel tells us that highly competitive heath plants are rife in the park's grasslands, as we saw on Taranaki Falls Track last week. After completing the walk, my sons and I hike to Tāwhai Falls, where a rainbow arcs over green water. A man swimming in clinging underwear below the falls whoops with shock at the cold water. Dainis rolls his eyes and turns away in embarrassment.

At the end of the park access road, I photograph a "kiwi crossing" road sign, and the kids and I check out ancient avalanche debris called the Mounds of the Murimoto Formation. The Mounds are visible as huge lumpy hummocks, overgrown with dense shrubs and flax. According to an interpretive sign, they consist of plates of layered rock that fell away from the northwest slope of Ruapehu following an earthquake thousands of years ago. Some of the pieces that broke off the mountain were *twelve kilometres deep* and remained intact while they slid *fourteen kilometres* across the landscape. The boys and I stare over the distance to Ruapehu. *How fast did the rock move? How long did it take for it to arrive here?* Again, my imagination staggers.

HOMESCHOOL FIELDTRIP TO TONGARIRO NATIONAL PARK

"Excuse me." I catch the attention of the receptionist in the visitor centre, to which we've returned on a trading mission. "We're from Canada. My sons collect coins, and my older son is particularly interested in an Australian coin with a kangaroo on it that's in your donation box. Would it be possible for him to trade a Canadian or New Zealand coin for it?"

The curly haired receptionist studies the boys and me. "Just a minute." She disappears into a back room and returns with a bulging cloth bag. She smiles and hands it to me. "The foreign coins are no good to us. We can't use them. I think there are a few roos in there."

My sons' smiles flash like startled sunlight. We thank the receptionist profusely. As I drive away from the park, with its volcanic peaks lost in building thunderstorms, Dainis and Jānis giggle and pass the bag back and forth as though it were filled with gold.

January 9

MORNING SUN dapples the forest with brown and brilliant green. Rain-wet shrub and fern leaves smear water onto Dainis's shoes and my boots. A male tomtit, dressed in North Island formal attire of black and white, inspects us as we approach, as though judging whether we shall be allowed to enter this particular forest ballroom, Ōhinetonga Lagoon. We greet the tomtit and check the stoat trap Dainis set near the lagoon two days ago in the hope he'd catch a rat to photograph. The trap is empty, but the peanut butter bait is gone. Dainis resets the trap, his hopes now centered on tomorrow.

We collect tracking tunnels from the scrub habitat along the river, and then from the forested area with its thick understory. "There are way more mice tracks than last time!" Dainis enthuses. "Eighty percent in the scrub, and twenty percent in the forest. This time, I even had more mice than rats in the scrub, and last time, there weren't any in the forest. There are more rats in the forest this time, too."

"Now do you see why it's a good idea to have different sites within the same habitat?" I ask.

He nods emphatically. "Yah. There's variation."

On the way to the next set of traps, we find two large snails with a checked pattern on their shells resting on a glistening mat of drying mucus beside the track. One of the snails has pulled the front half of its body up onto the head of the other.

"They're mating, I think," I hazard a guess.

Dainis frowns. "Doesn't one shoot a spear of stuff into the head of the other?"

"Something like that. I believe it's called a spermatophore."

"Look at the slime. *Eee-ew!*"

"That's how they move, on a trail of slime they produce. Of course, it's not really *slime*. It's mucus. You know how slippery mucus is. They just slide right along it."

"*Hmm.*" Dainis nods, his revulsion disappearing with understanding. We open the station wagon's rear hatch and prop it open with a sturdy, dried flax flowering stalk before dumping the twenty tunnels inside. Then, patiently, Dainis replaces the tracking papers where necessary and re-paints the bait panels with the thick mixture of greasy paraffin oil and charcoal. I help him thumbtack the clean papers and newly-blackened bait panels inside the corrugated plastic tunnels. Then we fold each tunnel flat and tape five into a bundle for easy carrying.

We cross Whakapapa River Bridge to set tunnels in a third site of scrub habitat, but stop abruptly on seeing a cream-coloured feral goat standing stock-still in the middle of the 42 Traverse. Its coat is ragged, and the hair on its withers stands erect as it observes us with wary curiosity before trotting into roadside shrubs. While Dainis sets five tunnels in scrub adjacent to the river, we're inspected by welcome swallows that skim above our heads. We can hear their young begging for food from within holes in a nearby cliff face.

We return across the bridge, and Dainis sets the remaining five scrub habitat tunnels beside Ōhinetonga Loop Track on the opposite side of the road from where he set his first tunnels. Then we continue along the loop track and set tunnels in a third site of thick forest habitat. As we work, Dainis grows progressively quieter and less enthusiastic. Again, we finish far later than anticipated, and again, he's ravenous.

DURING THE afternoon, my family returns to Tongariro National

Park, this time to hike Silica Rapids Track. A sign beside the trailhead informs us that the montane forest of stunted mountain beech we're about to enter received an aerial application of 1080 (poison bait) on November 6. That bait is undoubtedly aimed at rats and possums – both highly invasive species – and, secondarily, at stoats that eat poisoned rats.

Within the forest, native mistletoes drip cascades of orange-red blossoms from large beech trees. Tin sleeves wrapped around the trees' trunks protect the parasitic mistletoes from possum depredation. An interpretive sign informs us that mistletoe flowers attract *tūī* and bellbirds, both of which twist open the flowers' tips to drink the nectar within, pollinating the flowers as they do so.

We follow a rushing stream upslope and encounter slumps of soil and vegetation, evidence of the fragility of this environment where easily-eroded ash soils lie loosely atop old lava. Dwarf shrubs and grassland replace the mountain beech forest. In an alpine bog, sundews glisten like miniature red flames awaiting insect meals. Silica Rapids are creamy white terraces on the bed of Waikare Stream. An interpretive display informs us that the stream collects silica and aluminium from the volcanic andesite rock over which it tumbles. The rushing, turbulent water releases carbon dioxide to the air, creating the right chemistry for alumino-silicate to be deposited on the streambed; hence, the terraces' creamy colour.

Farther along the track, we encounter a lava flow that, according to another interpretive sign, spilled from the extinct Iwikau Crater on the summit of Ruapehu less than 15 000 years ago. The broken black slab has been colonized by grasses and low shrubs. From atop it, we gaze over the landscape to where Tongariro rises in shattered glory against a backdrop of billowing clouds. Ngāuruhoe perches on Tongariro's southern slope like an apprentice resting on the shoulder of its master. The massive bulk of Ruapehu towers over the other volcanoes. Around us, jutting black lava outcrops create stark, bizarre sculptures. In contrast, the Ring Plain stretches serene and dappled by afternoon sunlight and shadow.

We descend the mountainside through dense stands of grasses and heaths, skirting lava outcrops and a bog washed by deep pools of water. After our return to Whakapapa, we drive Bruce Road up the north slope of Ruapehu through Scoria Flats, a barren wasteland of volcanic scoria. The dark-coloured, light-weight rock is riddled with bubble holes. It was formed when gas-filled lava blasted from the volcano and subsequently cooled. The wasteland road leads us to the base of Whakapapa Ski Field and Iwikau Village at 1 630 metres. Here, scattered alpine plants cling to volcanic rubble, and ski lodges rear up from boulder fields like outposts in a hostile frontier.

January 10

THE FOREST within Ōhinetonga Scenic Reserve is still and humid, dull in the shade of its many trees. No sun shines above it this morning. A robin, itself all shadow and flickering movement, perches on a thin-stemmed sapling, as though it were a scout sent down by the legions of songbirds encamped in the canopy above. Again, Dainis finds no small mammal tracks in the tunnels he placed in open forest.

"Maybe there isn't anything for them to eat," he tells me, his brow puckered in thought. "They probably don't eat ferns." A note of speculation enters his voice. "I think there'll be some when we set them on the other side of the road. It's closer to the lagoon."

Ōhinetonga Lagoon lies still and serene, its green and grey reflections perfect, its thickly vegetated shore some mysterious utopia for rats. We set the ten open-forest tunnels well back from the lagoon, beneath trees as tall and shading as those on the other side of the bush road. Then we check the shoreline tunnels.

"There are tracks here!" Dainis shouts from the first.

We dodge vines, push aside fern fronds, and stumble over fallen logs in our search for the next and then the next orange flag hanging somewhere amidst the thick vegetation. Each tunnel, once found, elicits another satisfied exclamation from Dainis. Then, "Oh-oh. I remember this one," he mutters when we find a flag at the top of a sheer drop-off with a short incline above it. Undaunted, he scuttles down the slanted slope and grips a slender sapling that bends beneath his weight. He kicks out and drops the three metres to the lagoon edge.

"Yup. More tracks."

He tosses the tunnel up to me before climbing a slim, branching tree. When he stretches one leg out to place a foot on the top edge of the bank, I reach forward to grip his outstretched hand and tug him toward me as he jumps from the tree.

"Thanks!"

"Good thing you're a monkey!"

He laughs. "It's fun!"

Once we've collected the tunnels, we sit on the boardwalk that crosses the lagoon, with our shoes off and feet dangling over the water. The tracking papers are smudged with rats' black footprints and yellow urine stains. We change the papers, and Dainis squishes out more oil and charcoal "ink" from a shoe polish dispenser onto the central bait panels. "Why would there be so many rats here?" he ponders. "A hundred percent! And last time I had ninety percent."

We scan the lagoon's shoreline, with its overhanging trees, shrubs, and palm-leaf ferns. Dense clumps of sedges grow at the water line, some bearing seeds, as do some of the thick-stemmed rushes and other aquatic plants growing in the lagoon. "I wonder if rats swim for food," I remark. "There would be plenty of seeds."

"Stoats swim." Dainis stretches out on the boardwalk and leans over the edge to wash his hands in the lagoon. It's almost noon, so he munches on the sandwich he brought along. "The work goes better when I'm not hungry," he tells me almost apologetically. Like all researchers, he's learned that obtaining data comes at a personal cost. In his case, that cost is hunger resulting from hours of physical exertion in the outdoors.

DAINIS AND RAT TRACKS

While he eats, two long-tailed cuckoos wing across the lagoon and disappear in the rainforest. A white-faced heron screeches out its call and perches atop the tallest tree in sight. Ducks whir in a compact flock over the lagoon, then change direction abruptly when they spot us on the boardwalk.

We rise from our respite and tackle the lagoon edge jungle to set tunnels there for the third and last time. I awkwardly pace out the distance atop the steep slope above the water, where vines and ferns snare my feet. Abrupt rises and drops in terrain cause me to continually adjust my estimated metre-long steps. When we reach each thirty-metre mark, Dainis tosses down the bait containers before slipping and sliding down the slope after them to the level of the lagoon edge. I toss a tunnel down to him, which he baits and sets before scrambling back up the slope. The tenth and last tunnel is a fight all the way. We slog through mud and slip on moss- and liverwort-covered rocks. We pull ourselves up onto the bases of tree ferns to ascend vertical rises, then drop down again into hollows.

"Whew! We fought for every metre of that one," I pant.

Dainis grins. "Yeah. I liked it."

I see him standing beside me, his youth shining like a questing star seeking all that life can give. I see him happily scrambling up and down slippery slopes, reaching out with both hands to grasp each new climbing challenge as it arises. I see him go places I can't go, or won't go, and marvel that this child, whom I so often see as the quiet intellectual, also has the heart of an adventurer.

On our return to the house, Jānis bounces up and down on the porch, his eyes lit with excitement. "We caught another stoat!"

"Super! What's its name?" I ask.

"Samson!" Jānis dances about. "And I got to drive the quad almost all the time!"

I feel a jolt of surprise. "You did? Not on the Makos, I hope."

"No." His smile holds a tinge of disappointment. "And not in that place that you don't like." He shrugs nonchalantly. "But I got to drive between most of the traps. Not in the hard places and not when we drove fast to help Tala with the stoat."

VILIS EARTAGGING STOAT

Jānis heaves a sigh huge with joy, as though happiness blazed through him from the morning's adventures. "I'm really glad I went out with Vilis today."

While scrounging up a mid-day meal, I call out to Vilis, "So, how much did Samson weigh?"

"Two hundred and eighty-five grams."

"And the females are about…?"

"A hundred fifty to a hundred seventy."

"So, he's a mature male."

Vilis chuckles. "Yeah. And he sure smelled like a mature male, too."

Jānis grimaces. "He stank! *Blah!* Awful. Disgusting. Horrible."

So, the rank, musky smell of stoat, a rare perfume to a select few like Vilis, repels yet another novice to the world of mustelids.

During the evening, Vilis tells me, "You know, Jānis said that catching the stoat today made this North Island trip worthwhile for him. He said he liked watching Tala and me process it even more than driving the quad."

January 11

THIS MORNING, while Vilis and Dainis check stoat traps and collect tracking tunnels, Jānis and I tramp Whakapapanui Track, a six-kilometre trail near Whakapapa in Tongariro National Park. Wild wind rushes overhead, whipping the branches of mountain beeches and *kānuka* trees. Today, the volcanoes rise aloof and hidden, cloaked in rolling purple cloud, as if Tongariro might seek the council of Ngāuruhoe and Ruapehu in ruling his domain.

Sheltered by trees, Jānis and I walk briskly. At our sides, stunted and cluttered beech forest spills over with plant life: tiny-leaved twiggy coprosma, shining broadleaf, five-finger, umbrella fern, mosses and stiff grasses. Straight, ragged-barked *kānuka* punch through the beeches and shrubs, lifting flattened, needle-leaved branches into the wind. Mountain cabbage trees rustle their skirts of dead leaves. Yellow tear-drop beech leaves lie on the path beneath our feet, and red mistletoe flowers stain a boardwalk. Grey warblers, chaffinches, and silvereyes skulk in shrubs, their songs bright dashes of sound against the rushing wind and Whakapapanui Stream's tumbling gurgles.

Too soon we reach Whakapapa, then retrace our steps to the trailhead while the breath of Tongariro spits rain and chases tongues of blue smoke cloud across Ruapehu's slopes.

During the afternoon, my family stocks up on groceries and completes miscellaneous tasks in Taumarunui. "You know the Yamaha we have?" Vilis asks the proprietor of Honda First. "I'd arranged to return it this week. Can we have it for another week?" He knows Andrea Byrom will arrive four days from now and will require a quad.

"Yeah. No drama," the man tells Vilis. "I see you've got your ice creams."

We do indeed. Lime and Fruit Salad cones this time – relief from the heat that pulsates off the walls and streets of Taumarunui.

January 12

WHAKAPAPA RIVER runs clear and low, its sands stained the colour of rust. Ripples caused by Jānis's fishing lure spread a set of shimmering, silver-green concentric circles over the water's smooth flow. A *tūī* flies parallel to the opposite bank, its white *poi* stark against the bird's dark body and the green ferns growing on the bank.

Behind the *tūī*, the slope shows the face of Tongariro Forest. Slim trees rise through thick clumps of fern cascading down the steep incline. Lichen-bearded giants thrust trunks upward through the understory. Scattered clumps of *toetoe* toss out curved leaves. Tree ferns radiate messy heads of green fronds. All this stands above a rocky bank of cream-coloured pumice on this stretch of serene river called the Boat Hole.

Jānis steps onto a thick log to free his snagged lure and remains there to fish. He bobs his lure in and out among submerged rocks and repeatedly casts it out across the water. Sometimes it plops into the river a disappointing five metres from the reel; sometimes it sings out in a long arc to land two-thirds of the way across.

JĀNIS FISHING AT THE BOAT HOLE

"That's as much line as I have," Jānis tells me, and I hear a vulnerable, frustrated edge in his voice. It's there because for the second day in a row Dainis is with Vilis on the quad (because he missed quad time due to his Scout project) and will likely be allowed to drive it on this last day of our stoat research. Vilis and Tala – returned from her holiday – will close the stoat traps for the weekend, ending my husband's disappointingly unsuccessful involvement in the Tongariro Forest stoat project. (Eventually, the entire stoat project at this site was abandoned due to the low number of stoats.)

I sit on grey sand amid grasses and scattered blackberry canes, the view all green and grey: the vegetation and its reflection in the river, the rounded sky above me, the river strewn with rocks above and below this gentle place. Even Jānis, dressed in green rubber boots, grey-green cargo pants, and an old white T-shirt, blends in. I listen to the birds and watch a silvereye preen in a shrub beside me, the tiny songbird's dipping head drawing my attention to its white eye-ring, one of nature's captivating circles. I'm at peace, but I see frustration building in Jānis.

"We might as well go," he grumbles. "This river doesn't have any fish in it."

I know it's not the lack of fish that's bothering him. It's the fact that he's yearning to be riding a quad in the forest. "Jāni," I say gently, "fishing is about more than catching fish. It's about being out on the water and practicing your casting and enjoying the sights and sounds of the river."

"Not for me," he says tersely, his face tight with disappointment.

At times like this, I feel helpless. Unsure of what I can do to soothe my child. There's so much pain, such tenderness of aching spirit in youth. Yet, I know the river touched Jānis, for there were moments when he stood on bank or log with rod in hand, his lure singing out over the river decorated with the glorious reflection of a thousand leaves, and his face was filled with peace.

DURING THE afternoon, my family again drives to Taumarunui, and we decide to take in the movie *Space Cowboys* showing at the old Regent Cinema. In the theatre, the air is musty. The vinyl-covered seats are worn at the edges. Red-carpeted walls and floor are lit by four groupings of three hanging globe lights, yellow above red above blue. Music from the fifties sets my toes tapping while we wait for the lights to dim. It strikes me that the music is of the same vintage as the theatre. At first, the four of us think we may have a private showing; however, twenty minutes after the movie was scheduled to begin, ten other people are seated in widely-dispersed clusters within the theatre.

Ads appear on the movie screen, followed by previews. Then black-and-white film footage set in 1958 rolls onto the screen. It takes me a few seconds to realize that this is the feature film, and suddenly, it's all one. The theatre and movie. The mustiness and music. The slightly fuzzy voices of Clint Eastwood and Tommy Lee Jones arguing. The worn, vinyl seats. It's all part of a different movie in my mind, one about perception and remembering, about time passing and what we take from its passage and what we leave.

The same is true of our New Zealand adventure.

Then the movie jumps to 1998, and I, along with its heroes, am catapulted into modern space age technology.

January 13

A YELLOW-GREEN forest hangs beneath the surface of Ōhinetonga Lagoon. Pondweeds comprise this forest. Their curved stems push club-like flower spikes up into the light. An aquatic insect called a water boatman rows among the pondweeds, and I again paddle through their deceiving canopy on a slab of close-cell foam insulation. A week ago, we experimented with floating on the lagoon using foam slabs Vilis found under the DOC house. Instantly, the boys and I were hooked.

Vilis treads water in the lagoon and calls out, "These weeds are really tall. The water is over my head here."

Dainis and Jānis kick and splash aboard their foam platforms, gliding above the aquatic forest and below the terrestrial one on a rippling silver-green interface between sky and water. Around us, the reflections of rushes on the lagoon's surface form wavy green-and-red doodles beneath straight stalks. The artistic doodles and gentle motion of water against my paddling feet soothe me, washing away the frustration of an abandoned hike after lunch. I say "abandoned" because we couldn't find the track, even with four passes by the spot where the map indicated it should be.

This lagoon is a place out of time, a place where I'm caught up in wonder. It makes me stop and take my shoes off so I can dangle my feet over the water. It makes me find a way to float on its surface so I can drink in the motion of aquatic insects and the art that light creates on rippling water. And all the while, the rest of my existence is on hold.

Dark-bellied clouds drift over the lagoon. They block the sun's heat and hint at impending showers. Reluctantly, I break up the lagoon party. "If we're going to do that quadding, we'd better do it now before we get our daily thundershower."

The time has come for a last goodbye to the Tongariro Forest tracks, to the quads and curving, cutting *toetoe*. At the pumice quarry, "donuts" spun by skidding quad tires mark the quarry base. More bullet holes pock the sheer wall and puncture the trash littering the quarry floor. I trade places with Dainis, allowing him to drive Tala's work Honda. Vilis switched with Jānis on the Yamaha at the bridge.

The boys drive the broad section of the 42 Traverse carefully and climb rocky Water Supply Road with caution. My helmet visor periodically knocks against Dainis's helmet, and I soon discover that a quad passenger has a much bumpier ride than the driver. This realization gives me a new appreciation for the boys' patience and endurance these past four weeks. Beside us, the forest falls away to patches of field and bush veiled with blue haze. That haze beguiles me into thinking New Zealand is a vast country that extends far beyond this magnificent view.

Near the top of Water Supply Road, Jānis turns to me, his eyes bright with unusual interest. "So, Magi, are you going to come on the Mud Track?"

I hadn't intended to. "Why do you ask?"

"Because if you come, Vilis is more likely to drive through the mudholes."

Ah, yes. The second quad can help the first out of difficulties. Sticky, muddy difficulties. "So I can pull him out, you mean?"

"Yup."

"Let's walk it for a bit so I can have a look at it."

"We've seen the start of it before," Dainis reminds me.

"You had a trap in there, remember?" Vilis says. "You and Dainis walked in."

Now I recall…my first day of quadding…a huge mudhole…Vilis's quad tilting and lurching up the rutted track beyond the hole…Dainis and I deciding we'd walk. We also walked in when setting the two traps on Boxing Day.

As we check out Mud Track's first 200 metres on foot, Vilis stares at the trail in amazement. "It's almost *dry*. The last time I drove through here, it was mud all the way and water sloshing down the track ahead of me."

Perhaps I'm braver, perhaps more foolish. More likely, I'm simply more experienced than I was. To me, it doesn't look like anything I haven't already driven. "I'll give it a go."

Jānis grins with delight.

At its start, Mud Track mounds up like a red-ridged elephant's back. Then it transforms into a rough, twisting trail, like a muscular snake writhing through *toetoe* and thickets of blossoming *mānuka*. The quads cling to parallel ridges of red, hard-packed soil with deep hollows between. They slant along the trail with one wheel on a ridge and one in a hollow. They press into graceful, slicing clumps of *toetoe* to skirt deep holes and roar into mudholes there's no way around, with wheels churning. I follow Vilis's lead carefully, staying close, then lose him on a rare level stretch where he speeds ahead. When Dainis and I catch up, we find the other half of our family mired two-thirds of the way through a huge morass. Thick black muck rises half-way up the Yamaha's wheels. I glance around and notice a dry, bumpy path skirting the hole.

Vilis smiles sheepishly. "I guess if there's a path around a hole, there's a reason for it."

Jānis grins irrepressibly, not the least bit uncomfortable about being stuck in that embarrassingly large mudhole. "It's a good thing Maģi did come along!"

"It certainly is," Vilis agrees.

STUCK QUAD ON MUD TRACK

Vilis and I jostle the quad, and he digs hard-packed mud from beneath it. The boys run into the forest to cut a thick vine to use as a tow rope.

"Did you go through this hole for Jānis?" I ask my husband.

Again he smiles sheepishly. "Well, sometimes after you've done something, it's hard to know just why you did it."

After the boys return with a sturdy vine, I poke one end of its flexible length down through the metal bars that protect the front of the mired Yamaha. Vilis loops the other end through the bars at the back of the Honda. We knot the vine at each end, and then attempt to extract the Yamaha. I climb onto the stuck quad. Dainis mounts the Honda. Vilis is ready to pull on the vine. When he gives the signal, Dainis turns on the gas. The Honda rears up like a horse, its front wheels swinging up and backwards.

"*No, no, no!*" I shout.

Vilis looks up and pushes Dainis forward. "Put on the brake!" he yells, and Dainis does so, dropping the quad safely back to the ground.

"I should have remembered that from Tractor 101," Vilis mutters, removing the vine from the Honda's bars and repositioning it around its axle. "I tied it too high. That's how tractors flip over onto their drivers."

Shaken, we try again, this time with Jānis, who's the lightest of us, on the Yamaha, and with me driving the Honda. Engines roar. Blue exhaust spurts. Vilis yells instructions. In the midst of it all, the Yamaha breaks free and crawls forward through the heavy, clinging mud until its front wheels are out of the hole.

"We couldn't have done that in Canada," Dainis pipes up excitedly from the dry path beside the mudhole. "No vines there!"

Farther along Mud Track, the trail writhes into steep, gouged hills, bringing us face-to-face with eroding red soil. Now the forest is above us, rather than beside us. The quads buck, pitch, and claw their way up the snake's gut on the kind of track I've never driven. I'm in over my head. The Honda I'm driving fights its way out of a deep hole and lurches crazily as it starts to climb the dirt wall to my left. The quad is completely off balance, its right front wheel and left rear wheel spinning in air, the latter over the mudhole. The machine begins to tilt to the left, so I brake and jam a foot against the dirt wall to stop the quad from falling over onto Dainis and me and crushing us against the wall.

"I'm getting off!" Dainis yells.

"Yes, get off!"

My heart thuds as Dainis scrambles off the back of the Honda and runs down the slope out of harm's way. With just two of the quad's wheels touching the earth's surface and the machine's weight balanced against me, I'm very much aware of how powerful and dangerous the machine is. Slowly, I release the brake with no throttle on, hoping the Honda will slip backward far enough down the slope to put me on more level ground. As it inches back, I start to lose my balancing foot-brace against the wall. I jam on the brakes and call to Vilis for help.

He leaves the Yamaha parked at the top of the slope, slips between the wall and me, and takes over. First, he attempts the same manoeuvre I tried. When that fails, he wrestles the Honda sideways off the wall and back onto the track.

"I should have done that right away," he says, again chiding himself.

"You can take it to the top," I tell him. I have no desire whatsoever to tackle the rest of that menacing, eroded hill.

At the top of the slope, we drive with heightened caution, skirting gaping holes when we can. A loud, metallic clunk startles us when Vilis drives through the shallow edge of a hole. The noise, which comes from beneath the Yamaha, doesn't disappear and instead grows louder when he steers the quad onto dry ground. "Doesn't sound good." He peers under the Yamaha. "Well, that's it. It won't be going any farther today. The universal joint is shot. We'll have to leave it."

"How will it get back?" I ask.

"The dealer said they'd make repairs anywhere. I'll call him tonight to let him know what happened, so they can have it fixed by the time Andrea arrives. They have a mechanic in Ōwhango."

"Good thing it didn't happen when you were stuck!" Jānis says.

"Yes, that is a good thing." Vilis parks the Yamaha within a small level area in a stand of stunted *mānuka* growing beside the track. Then he looks at the boys and me. "So, what do we do now?"

I spread my hands. "I'm perfectly happy to walk out."

"What about the boys?"

"We can both go on the back," Jānis suggests.

I veto that.

"Then we can take turns," Jānis offers.

Vilis shakes his head. "I don't think that will work."

"Take my quad and go get the car," I say in my brooking-no-argument voice. I've had my fill of quadding. "You can meet us at the bottom of Water Supply Road. We'll walk out."

"But I'll be back long before you get down."

"I don't think so. It's what? Three kilometres? And it's all down hill."

"But I want to *go*," Jānis insists, loathe to give up any chance to ride a quad.

"Vilis can drive faster alone," I say.

"That's true, I can." Vilis mounts the Honda.

"Then I'm just going to stay *here*!"

"Fine. You just stay here," I say, calling my son's bluff. I know this forest holds no dangers for him. New Zealand has no large carnivores that might attack him, or poisonous snakes that might bite him. And Jānis knows better than to eat any of the plants. When he's ready, he'll follow.

Vilis roars away, and Dainis and I jog and slide down the slippery red slope, helmets swinging from our hands. "I think we can walk this almost as fast as we drove it on the quads," I say.

"*Hmm*. Maybe. We had to slow down so much for all the holes."

The relief of not having to drive any more of the devouring track buoys my spirits. "So, what did you think of the Mud Track?" I ask Dainis, listening for movement behind us. I'm sure Jānis will come.

"Interesting." Dainis takes a few more steps before adding, "It was scary when the quad reared up."

"Yes, it was." For me, it was terrifying. Yet, we coped with the situation. Just like we're coping with a broken-down quad. Years ago, every night before I fell asleep, my mind would torment me with potential sources of danger and injury to my sons. Accidents. Poisonings. Deadly diseases. *What if this had happened? What if that hadn't happened? What if…*One night, in a blessed moment of clarity, I realized my projected fears were a form of self-inflicted torture. Then and there, I put up a wall against them, and I do my best to maintain it. Otherwise, life is too frightening.

Dainis and I creep around the big mudhole at the slope's base, its red water splashed onto the soil by Vilis on the Honda. We hear footsteps approaching from behind, and Jānis runs by. I relax. On a level stretch of the track, *toetoe* catches at our legs, but I don't care. We're safe, my feet are on solid ground, the rain is holding off, and blossoms of Himalayan honeysuckle dangle from roadside shrubs like tiered burgundy bells.

At the bottom of Water Supply Road, my kids and I strike out on the 42 Traverse, pausing to admire a thick grove of tree ferns we always sped past on the quads. A quartet of mountain bikers passes us with brief glances and greetings. Soon after, we hear a car and spot the bright blue of the Bomb. Like co-conspirators, my sons and I grin at Vilis's open-mouthed surprise when he sees us.

January 14

FOR THE third and last time, Dainis collects his tracking tunnels from the open forest and lagoon-edge habitats. Rats chewed on the sides or bases of many of the tunnels and deposited footprints in 100 percent of the lagoon-edge tunnels and 30 percent of the open-forest tunnels. Thus ends my older son's sampling of the four habitats within Ōhinetonga Scenic Reserve.

Late in the morning, we all head for Ōhakune and Blyth Track on Ruapehu's south slope. We want a gentle outing today because we're saving our energy to tackle the Tongariro Alpine Crossing, in Tongariro National Park, tomorrow. That track, often simply referred to as the Tongariro Crossing, has a reputation as the finest one-day tramp in New Zealand. It's a nineteen-kilometre, all-day ascent, traverse, and descent of Tongariro's massive volcanic peak. It'll be our most challenging tramp to date, and we're keen to pit our hiking skills against it.

In Ōhakune, we pause to picnic in a park, where Dainis and Jānis clamber over an old army tank. Jānis shouts, "Hey, Vilis! *This* is what we needed on the Mud Track!"

Vilis and I pack up the remains of our picnic, after which we all climb into the car and drive halfway up Ōhakune Mountain Road to the start of Blyth Track, originally cut in the early twentieth century. The current tramping trail is narrow and bordered by red beech with sharply-toothed, oval leaves. Old, mud-covered corduroy logs from the original track (which traversed bogs)[37] are slippery beneath our feet. The clinging barbs of bush lawyer catch at our clothes and skin. Clumps of mountain flax and mounds of umbrella ferns clutter the track edges. Brilliant green mosses carpet a fallen tree trunk, and delicate ferns grow in small crevices in the trunk or sprout from its top in artistic compositions.

After an hour of strolling, we reach the bridge across Mangawhero River where we sit with our feet dangling over the water, in still and silent contemplation of tomorrow's climb up, over, and down Te Heuheu Tūkino IV's beloved mountain. The river beneath us runs low and quiet. The air smells good, cool, and strangely like autumn.

We rouse ourselves and retrace our steps, then drive to Mangawhero Falls Track. From the track, we see flamboyant red-flowering mistletoes cascading down beech trunks, and a delicate waterfall spilling onto dark rock. Then we drive farther up the mountain to where bare Turoa Ski Field lies as bleak and strewn with scoria as is Iwikau Village on the other side of the volcano.

January 15

POSSIBLE RISKS: sunburn, get blown off cliff, get rained on, dehydration, slip down a cliff.
Precautions: use sunscreen, go on a calm day, bring raincoat, bring lots of water, don't go when tired.

At 6:00 a.m., clear sky signals fine weather for our all-day tramp of the Tongariro Alpine Crossing, which will be Dainis's second outdoor adventure aimed at earning the Explorer badge in Scouting, and will kick off two weeks of vacation before we return to Lincoln. We eat a hearty breakfast and fill daypacks with light jackets, hats, sunscreen, snacks, lunch, and water bottles, then drive to Whakapapa. The line-up for the bus to the Mangatepopo Road trailhead of the famous track soon stretches over a hundred people long. "This tramp is going to be way too crowded," Vilis mutters as we board the bus.

Seated at the back of the bus, I glance out windows at passing scenery and chat with two Kiwi men dressed in running attire. I notice a clean volcanic cone rising high into the sky in the southwest. "Is that Taranaki?" I ask the older of the two men, a grizzled character carrying only a small waist pack and drink bottle.

" 'Taranaki' to the tourists," he responds dryly. " 'Egmont' to the locals."

"How long have they been using 'Taranaki'?" I ask.

"Ten or fifteen years?" he asks the other man, who is lean, dark, and younger.

"That's about right."

When we disembark from the bus, the grizzled runner grins. "Should be back in time for a late game of golf."

At the trailhead, grasses blanket the soil. They're interspersed with greenish-white mosses. In the distance, the grasses give way to ground-hugging alpine vegetation and black lava outcrops backed by the spreading bulk of Tongariro, which I've learned is a volcanic complex composed of a dozen or more cones.[38] Near the apex of Mangatepopo Valley, a splash of neon green spills from the base of a plunging slope. On the valley floor, a braided stream shines like silver ribbons in the sunlight.

We tramp up the valley and cross the stream on a side trail to investigate the neon green splash, which is Soda Springs. As we approach the springs, the rotten-egg stench of hydrogen sulphide pervades the air. Water trickles and drips over a lava ledge. It forms a miniature waterfall, the droplets refracting light into a misty rainbow. Thick pads of mosses, tufts of grasses, and wildflowers, including yellow buttercups and white ourisias, cling to the wet rock. They're nourished by the trickling water that runs down slope and sustains a broad delta of bright-green grasses. Beyond the wet grasses, scattered clumps of white-flowering herbs dot coarse, crushed scoria on the valley floor.

We cross the grass delta by hopping from rocks to grass hummocks, then follow the side trail back to the main track. A line of people ahead of us snakes upward on the boulder-strewn flank of Tongariro. Behind us, another line of people extends toward the car park, with a few trampers joining the queue after visiting Soda Springs. Vilis was right. There are *way* too many people on this tramp.

As we climb to the saddle between Tongariro and Ngāuruhoe, our feet fight for purchase on loose rock, and our hands grasp at lumps of lichen-covered lava. Jānis slips and falls, bringing tears, so we rest on an outcrop – the volcanoes black and brown and barren beside us. Some of the more adventurous trampers, including the two runners I chatted with on the bus, turn onto a side trail and attack a steep scree slope that leads to Ngāuruhoe's peak.

Beyond the saddle, we remain on the main track and step onto South Crater, a circular orange-yellow plain dotted with rocks and colonized by clumps of tufted grasses on its outer edges. Desolate is the only word to describe it; however, its level surface gives us a break from climbing.

From the crater floor, the track leads us onto a ridge between South Crater and a vast, circular moonscape comprised of ragged rock ridges interspersed with seas of smooth dust. This, we decide, must be Red Crater.

Cold wind stings my bare legs while we eat bagged lunches in the lee of a massive orange boulder beside a cliff that drops into the moonscape. To the south, Ngāuruhoe towers over us, its crater rim stained red and white. Central Crater is a barren brown plain marked by a black lava tongue. It lies to the north. To the west, Tongariro's summit soars above South Crater's level bed. Small figures of other trampers increase in size as they approach the ridge. Some use walking sticks. One hiker is a wee girl I guess to be no more than six years old. She scampers up the ridge, chattering cheerfully.

Rested and refuelled, we climb the ridge, which narrows into an arch of rock and pumice sand. From this vantage point, we peer down into a gaping hole encircled by a curved wall of red and black rock. A gigantic dyke protrudes from the crater wall, the lava chute's heat-fused walls sagging like soft wax.

"*That's* Red Crater," Dainis pronounces, and we realize we're standing atop its rim. Unlike the eroded moonscape and the South Crater, softened by plant invasion, Red Crater is raw and immediate, a reminder that Tongariro's volcanic heart still beats. Ash issued from this crater in 1926.[39] And Ngāuruhoe, which looks like an independent peak, is in fact Tongariro's main active vent. During the past 150 years, Ngāuruhoe has spewed ash seventy times, most recently in 1975.[40] (In 2012, long after our New Zealand adventure, Tongariro erupted twice, sending plumes of smoke high into the sky and blanketing the Central Volcanic Plateau with ash.)[41]

We step carefully to the rim's highest point, aware we're only metres away from tumbling off the edge into Red Crater's gaping maw.

THIS DARK SHELTERING FOREST

EMERALD LAKES, TONGARIRO ALPINE CROSSING

Beyond this point, which is the highest on the Tongariro Alpine Crossing, a stunning vista of volcanic features greets us to the north. Three small Emerald Lakes lie below us. Blue Lake occupies a plateau to the northwest. North Crater's flat-topped upland rises west of Blue Lake. The spreading water of Lake Taupō, so immense we at first think it's the ocean, stretches away in the distance. The craters and vividly coloured lakes surrounding us manifest an other-worldly aura, one of barren desolation, smouldering power, and toxic beauty.

Jānis and Dainis grin as we scree-slide down the ridge from the crater's rim. Beside us, wafts of steam, reeking of hydrogen sulphide, veil a whitish, deadly looking slope. We skirt the stinking slope and tramp past two of the Emerald Lakes. Their water fills old explosion craters and is impossibly green. Its brilliant, gemlike colour is derived from minerals washed down from the white slope.[42]

From the exquisite vista of the Emerald Lakes, the track twists down onto Central Crater, a lifeless plain of brown pulverized rock marred by an old lava flow from Red Crater. Cold wind whips us as we follow a poled route across the crater.

VILIS AND JĀNIS ON CENTRAL CRATER; RED CRATER BEHIND THEM

The two runners jog by. "Hi! How's your day going?" the grizzled runner asks.

"Good. How's yours?" I respond.

"Good. Ngāuruhoe was high."

"I'll bet it was."

From the northern edge of Central Crater, we climb to the plateau occupied by broad turquoise Blue Lake, which fills one of Tongariro's old volcanic vents.[43] We skirt the lake and stare at the spreading vastness of Lake Taupō beneath a sky draped in mauve and frilled with brilliant white cloud. Jānis spots an island we saw during our visit to the Morse bach in December, and we notice a volcanic peak with three cusps to the north of the lake.

Beyond Blue Lake, which is sacred to the local Māori tribe, the Ngāti Tūwharetoa, we begin our descent. White-green mosses, tufts of short, fine grasses, herbaceous plants with bell-shaped flowers, and prostrate dwarf shrubs compete for space on Tongariro's northern slope. As we tramp farther down the mountain, tussock grasses intermingle with the alpine plants. At lower elevations, red tussock grass is the dominant vegetation. When we pause for a rest, the grass's red-gold fans almost obscure Dainis as he explores off the trail.

After our stop, we tramp gentle switchbacks downhill to Ketetahi Hut and Ketetahi Stream. Alongside the stream, a steaming slope pocked with gas vent holes borders the track. Mineral-stained clays on the stream's banks, along with vivid green algae growing on the milky water, create a gaudy geothermal art show in outlandish shades of purple, orange, green, and burgundy. Rocks on the slope feel warm to our touch. Vilis reaches out to test the temperature of escaping gases. "Ow!" he yelps, yanking back his hand. "That's hot!" The reek of the gases turns our stomachs, so we hurry past the hut and the trampers resting on its deck. Some are likely planning to spend the night.

Below Ketetahi Hut, a golden expanse of grassland waves in the wind, broken only by clouds of steam billowing up from behind a hill. That steam signals the presence of Ketetahi Hot Springs, and we catch whiffs of a sulphurous stench carried from the springs to us on the wind. The track curves around the hillside and offers us a distant view of the springs. Slopes stained green, pink, and white with minerals plunge in sharp angles, as though a mighty axe had slashed a broad cleft in the mountain. The steam plumes upward from their base. Although within the national park, the hot springs are on sacred land in a small enclave of Māori-owned land, not open to the public.

Below the springs, countless jarring wooden steps that had been set into the ground to reduce erosion, lead us down slope through more grassland. Then we drop into a cool, refreshing forest and are deceived into thinking we've almost reached our destination, only to discover, on exiting the forest, that the track continues on through more grassland. With Tongariro's treasures behind us, the remainder of the tramp becomes an endurance test. Our feet ache, exhaustion dogs us, and Jānis falls again, scraping his arm and again in tears. It's been a tough tramp for him.

At 5:00 p.m., eight hours after setting out from the Mangatepopo Road parking area, we reach Ketetahi car park. Other trekkers, some tinged with sunburn, sit on benches beneath shelters, waiting for buses and vans to arrive to transport them back to Whakapapa. When a van arrives, I approach the driver. "Excuse me. Would you know when the next bus to Whakapapa will arrive?"

"Tomorrow," he tells me.

My jaw drops. "Do you mean there isn't another one this evening?"

He takes pity on me. "Six o'clock."

We share a laugh and I return to the shelter to sit beside Vilis. Jānis slumps against me and closes his eyes, exhausted. Dainis sits at our feet, cross-legged on the wooden deck. He rummages in his pack and happily pulls out the copy of *Huckleberry Finn* he carried over the mountain to relieve the boredom of the bus rides. This first day of our vacation will be hard to beat.

ON TONGARIRO ALPINE CROSSING

January 16

STATION WAGON packed? Check. Boys in the car? Check. When Vilis and I open the Bomb's front doors, we're greeted by two posies of red clover, yellow hawkweed, and white and mauve yarrow, one on each front seat.

"Thank you!" We beam at our sons, and they grin back. Behind the boys, the car is filled with camping gear and backpacks holding enough personal supplies for ten days of exploring northern North Island. Vilis and I set the posies on the dash and climb into our seats, about to embark on part two of our North Island experience.

As Vilis drives us north past Taumarunui, rain streaks the

windows, creating a liquid screen that smears the landscape into near invisibility. "This drive doesn't seem real to me," he says. "Maybe it's because I can't see much." After a pause he decides, "It's hilly."

I stare at the rain-shrouded landscape, with its knife-edge hills grazed by sheep and cattle, and so steep you could never put a tractor on them. "*Mmm*. The hills are like ghosts appearing out of the mist."

When I glance ahead, I see sheep muzzles and wool tufts poking out of holes in a stock trailer pulled by a semi. The truck's wheels spray huge sheets of water off the highway. Behind us, a driver far too blasé about current road conditions sits on our tail. In the downpour, Te Kuiti is no more than a blur of buildings. Here, only thirty kilometres northeast of Paemako, where feisty, young May Tarrant, the real-life heroine of Phyllis Johnston's *Black Boots and Buttonhooks*, climbed a tree on her English family's homestead to sit in her nest in a *kiekie* clump,[44] we can discern nothing of our surroundings.

"In some ways it's good that I can't see out the back window," Vilis tells me.

"How's that?" I ask.

"Then I can't see the tailgaters."

We turn off the highway at Ōtorohanga, relieved to no longer share the rain-washed road with speeding drivers. Rather than erect our tent in pouring rain, we rent a caravan (camping trailer) for the night. Belatedly, we realize that the caravan park is situated beside the Ōtorohanga Kiwi House and Native Bird Park, a happy discovery. Vilis and the boys visit a *pūkeko* pacing back and forth inside the park fence.

"It pecked us!" Jānis reports.

"Then it stuck its head through the fence and let us stroke its neck feathers," Dainis adds. "They're purple and blue."

"I thought the red on its head was feathers," Vilis tells me, "but it's not. It's skull. That's a bald bird."

The rain stops, and evening beckons us to stroll peaceful Ōtorohanga streets. Damp sights and smells offer rich invitations to the senses. We hear the sounds of a band practising inside a small hall. Harmonious male and female voices sing into the evening air. Children dance past the hall's open doorway.

BEFORE BEDTIME, Vilis opens Elsie Locke's *A Canoe in the Mist* to read aloud to our sons. From the book's opening chapters, he draws forth the village of Te Wairoa with its 1886 blend of Māori tradition and Pākehā enterprise. Located on the shore of Lake Tarawera near Rotorua, the village was a mecca for tourists from around the world who travelled there to tour the Pink and White Terraces – glistening natural stairways of precipitated minerals that held warm pools. The terraces covered acres and rippled down a hillside thirty metres high adjacent to nearby Lake Rotomahana. One morning, however, mysterious waves slid over the calm surface of Lake Tarawera. Boat tourists and a Māori guide saw an ancient canoe caught in sunlight on the misty water. It was a *waka wairua,* a ghost canoe.[45]

Vilis pauses. Our sons have fallen asleep. We listen to their young-boy snores for a few moments, then lie content in each other's arms while streetlight filters through the blue caravan curtains and wild screams of kiwi tear the night.

January 17

IN THE morning, we tour Ōtorohanga Kiwi House and Native Bird Park, a showplace of rare and endangered native birds and reptiles. Within a huge, dome-shaped aviary planted with native vegetation, we spot a red-crowned parakeet (*kākāriki*). It looks like a splash of jade and fire on a slim branch. A heavy-bodied New Zealand pigeon (*kereru*) perches on a thicker branch, its plumage iridescent lilac and emerald. Brown flightless *weka* (rail and crake bird family) scurry under cover in a wetland. Trim *pūkeko* stride forth in classic blue and black, their white undertail feathers catching the eye with every step. Within one of many smaller aviaries, a *kākā* (one of New Zealand's three native parrot species) bathes in a pool, its curved upper mandible like a sickle arcing into the water. When the forest parrot spreads its broad bronze wings, they reveal ruby underwing feathers.

RED-CROWNED PARAKEET (*KĀKĀRIKI*)

After touring the aviaries, we enter the darkness of the Nocturnal Kiwi House. Perched high in a corner, a brown-feathered morepork issues its plaintive, begging *"more-pork"* request. Artificial moonlight spills onto shrubs and leaf litter below the owl and brightens a male brown kiwi's cape of soft, wispy feathers. The kiwi's bill is long and narrow with nostrils at the tip and whiskers at the base. The flightless bird's eyes are small and dark, and its vestigial wings are stumpy and unobvious. No tail protrudes through the kiwi's feather cape. The male strides on thick, sturdy legs that end in strong, clawed feet. All the while, the kiwi swings its long bill from side to side like a blind man swinging a white cane to test surfaces. Repeatedly, it probes leaf litter with its elongated bill, its keen sense of smell enabling the kiwi to locate food such as worms, grubs, and beetles (we're told this by a guide), as well as strips of ox heart and fruits provided by park staff.

A female kiwi steps into view from behind a mound of soil and leaves. Larger than the male, this bird has a longer, slightly curved bill. We're told that both kiwi are three years old and are approaching mating age. We're also told that wild brown kiwi are active for only four hours each night, from roughly 9:00 p.m. to 1:00 a.m. When the two kiwi call out, the male's cry is the high piercing scream we heard last night and in the darkness in Ōwhango. The female's call is a low, scratchy rattle.

Māori legend tells us that Kiwi lost his wings when he alone of the birds that flew in the sky volunteered to save the forests. The woodlands were sick, and Tāne Mahuta, lord of the forest, in turn asked Tūī, Pūkeko, Pipiwharauroa (shining cuckoo), and Kiwi to save the forests. In order to do that, the bird hero must leave the treetops, live on the forest floor, and eat the bugs attacking the trees. After looking down on the dark, damp earth so far below, the first three birds refused; however, brave Kiwi agreed. Tāne Mahuta warned Kiwi, "...do you realize that if you do this, you will have to grow thick, strong legs so that you can rip apart the logs on the ground and you will loose your beautiful coloured feathers and wings so that you will never be able to return to the forest roof? You will never see the light on day again." The legend tells us that Kiwi held to his agreement, sacrificing his life of flight and colour to save the forest. "But you Kiwi," Tāne Mahuta told him, "because of your sacrifice, you will become the most well known and loved bird of them all."[46]

After we exit the artificial kiwi habitat, we check out a display comparing bird egg sizes. As its centrepiece, the exhibit features a kiwi skeleton, and a kiwi egg on a bed of wood shavings between the skeleton's fleshless legs. After Jānis's excited description of an x-ray showing an egg inside a kiwi (which he saw during a Cub outing to Willowbank Wildlife Reserve in Christchurch in November) I shouldn't be surprised. However, the egg's size proportional to the skeleton is truly astounding, as though every internal organ must be displaced by its presence and the female's body nearly torn asunder by its passage to the outside world.

Only in a land with no terrestrial carnivores could such an egg have evolved. Unfortunately, therein lies the crux of the kiwi's downfall. This bird is flightless. It's almost blind. It's not huge and powerful like an ostrich or cassowary, those larger flightless birds of Africa and Australia. It's only active at night, and it lays its eggs, these massive, long-incubated eggs, in tunnels in the ground. All these factors make kiwi prime targets for nocturnal mammalian predators like stoats, which had not yet been introduced here when this country was still a land of birds. Unfortunately, stoats are currently all too real and abundant. How many more decades will the cry of the kiwi ring out over New Zealand's forests?

"Say, look at this!" I call Vilis and the boys over to a display containing a report of a kiwi research study that employed radio-telemetry. "It says 'data were analyzed using Locate II, the standard method.' " I grin at Vilis, and our sons laugh. Their father developed this computer program designed to triangulate radio-telemetry bearings and pinpoint the locations of radio-collared animals. Even though his stoat research didn't pan out, some of Vilis's earlier work has been used in studies of New Zealand's beleaguered national bird.

Early in the afternoon, we drive north from Ōtorohanga through lush farmland that supports dairy herds, corn fields, and the first serious hedges we've seen since Canterbury. In hillier country north of Hamilton, sheep reappear. A hundred kilometres north of Hamilton, Auckland sweeps up from the land in a shining spread of urban silver edged in the blue of the Tasman Sea to the west and that of the Pacific Ocean to the east. The Sky Tower's silver needle soars amid downtown skyscrapers, and Auckland Harbour Bridge arches ten lanes wide over Waitemata Harbour. On the water below, wind-filled sails billow above sleek hulls, as though urging freedom to boats tucked against the shoreline, or moored in marinas. Auckland, 'City of Sails.'

A half-hour's drive north of the city, we take the exit for Ōrewa on the Pacific coast. At Puriri Park campground, the receptionist Elaine welcomes us as friends, directs us to everything we need, and books us a ferry to Tiritiri Mātangi, an island bird sanctuary, for tomorrow morning.

We pitch our tent beside a stand of bamboo ten metres tall. The boys climb among the stalks and gather broken pieces from the ground. Peafowl cruise through the campground, and a creamy-beige Barbary dove – a rare African introduction, small and delicate in comparison with the heavy, iridescently plumaged New Zealand pigeon – "*coo-crooos*" from a tree. A trail within Alice Eaves Scenic Reserve, across Nukumea Stream from the campground, leads us among *nīkau* palms of every size, as well as among the straight boles of young *kauri* trees that tower above the canopy of palm leaves. Vilis nods to the *kauri*. "I can see how they'd want to use those for masts."

He's referring to Europeans who plundered *kauri* forests of northern North Island in the nineteenth and early twentieth centuries. Blinded by greed, they cut trees for masts, ship-building, and house construction, exporting vast quantities of timber until no more than scattered patches of the straight-boled giants remained. The forests, also decimated by land-clearing fires, shrank from occupying three million acres when Europeans arrived in New Zealand, to less than 5 percent of that area. In the mid-twentieth century, New Zealand's government banned *kauri* logging on crown land, thus allowing remaining stands of the slow-growing, fire-intolerant giants to begin to regenerate.[47]

When night falls, we slide into our sleeping bags. Creaking bamboo and the haunting, childlike screams of peafowl splinter the warm evening air around us.

January 18

SPUMES OF frothy wake leap into the air as the *Sea Cat* ferries us four kilometres from Gulf Harbour on the Whangapāraoa Peninsula near Ōrewa to the Scientific Reserve of Tiritiri Mātangi, "A Place Tossed by the Wind." Low in profile, the island presents a face of dense woodland and is an open sanctuary for some of New Zealand's rarest and most endangered birds.

The *Cat* disgorges us onto a long dock, and we enter the reserve in the company of a dozen other birders keen to explore this conservation success story. After more than a century of farming destroyed nearly all of the native forest on this 220-hectare island, a conservation plan was put in place to re-establish native forest and establish populations of rare birds. Free of stoats, the island offered a perfect opportunity to create a predator-free sanctuary accessible to the public. Polynesian rats (a legacy of the Māori settlement of the island) were eliminated by poisoning. Volunteers planted native woodland species to re-establish forest on 60 percent of the island. The remaining grassland was left to provide habitat for *takahē* and other grassland birds.[48]

Instructed to stay on the tracks, we explore the island's various habitats: shaded forest, scrubland, grassland, beach. Here, humans are the confined species, and it's the birds that study us freely.

In open scrubland, saddlebacks with black bodies and rust-coloured saddles and tail bases leap from branch to branch. They vocalize bold, ringing calls and eye us curiously. A *kōkako* with startling cerulean wattles hanging from its chin skulks in dense forest, its grey body and black-masked head almost hidden by foliage. Stitchbirds visit a nectar feeder in the forest. A male perches on the feeder ledge with his tail cocked and his black-velvet head sewn with a white "stitch" of erectile feathers behind each eye. Both saddlebacks and stitchbirds are extinct on the New Zealand mainland. *Kōkako* once lived in beech and mixed-wood forests throughout much of the country. Now they only live on a few islands and in mature podocarp forests in northern North Island.[49] Thus, Tiritiri Mātangi offers us a gift from the past.

We spot tiny brown quail, an Australian introduction, among the leaves on the forest floor, and Jānis catches a glimpse of a hedgehog. A red-crowned parakeet flies overhead when we hike through a coastal flax swamp. Flightless *takahē* lumber over grassland. They resemble awkward, turkey-sized *pūkeko*. Once thought extinct, *takahē* were rediscovered in 1948 in Fiordland on South Island. The twenty birds on Tiritiri Mātangi represent 10 percent of the world's population. The remainder are still found in their natural mountain grassland and beech forest habitats in Fiordland or were translocated to other offshore, predator-free islands.[50] Here, a single fluffy black juvenile forages on grasses amid a half-dozen adults, providing evidence that the Tiritiri Mātangi population is slowly increasing.

ADULT TAKAHĒ

White-fronted terns cruise above us as we follow a track to the beach. On the rock-and-shell shore, we find a dead blue penguin and observe living penguins incubating eggs in man-made rock burrows with glass tops. "Remember the blue penguins we saw coming ashore at Oamaru?" I ask, referring to a stop we made at the coastal town during our road trip from Lincoln to Queenstown in late November.

"Yeah! They swam like fish," Jānis says.

Vilis shakes his head. "I still can't believe they climbed those cliffs."

In mid-afternoon, the *Sea Cat* returns to ferry us to the mainland. As we speed away from Tiritiri Mātangi, each metre of the ferry's frothing wake seems to me to be a rung on a ladder that extends back toward this small approximation of what was once a land of birds.

January 19

BALD SUN accompanies us north from Ōrewa, where last night we again slept in our tent beside the bamboo wall, and where Jānis this morning collected two exquisite tail feathers dropped by a peacock parading through the campground.

At Warkworth, we take a secondary highway to Leigh and then a road to nearby Goat Island Marine Reserve. Warm tide pools on rock ledges beside a beach entice us to explore. We lean over surge channels biting into the ledges and are captivated by blue *maomao* and other colourful fishes that weave serpentine patterns in the clear water. They make us yearn to join them.

"Are we going to try snorkelling?" Jānis begs.

"What do you think, Dainis?" Vilis asks.

Dainis nods, making it thumbs up from all of us.

We drive to a nearby rental shop to kit ourselves out with shorty wetsuits, masks, snorkels, and flippers. None of us are familiar with wetsuits, and I first pull mine on backward. Jānis gives himself a wedgie trying on a suit that's too small. Dainis looks shocking in neon pink and green, the only remaining suit that fits him. Vilis and I rent prescription masks that enable us to see clearly (we both wear glasses).

"We've never snorkelled before," I tell the rental shop manager.

The tanned woman laughs. "You've picked the best site in New Zealand for your first go!"

We return to the beach and experiment in shallow, turbid water kicked up by a horde of swimmers. Beyond the beach area, clear water invites us to strike out into a narrow channel that separates the mainland from Goat Island. A forested lump of rock, the island has prominent intertidal ledges on its south end, about 300 metres offshore. I'm not much of a swimmer and tense up at the thought of swimming that expanse. But there's no way I'm going to let Vilis and the boys, all perfectly at home in water, go without me.

My heart pounds with anxiety as we snorkel away from the beach, but I soon discover that my flippers act as lazy, effective propellers that push me along smoothly at the water's surface. My anxiety melts away. We've been granted a thrilling new freedom, and the view through our masks reveals an amazing underwater world.

We trace the edge of the mainland rock ledges and swim in the surge channels, where *maomao* are living streaks of hot blue that swirl past our eyes and fingers. Smaller blue demoiselles and big pink snapper with blue spots cruise by and tempt us out into the channel. Large red *moki* with dark-red stripes cruise by. Magenta snails, sponges, and kelps inhabit the channel bottom. Vilis and Jānis, the thrill seekers in my family, dive for closer looks at sandy rock flats, kelp gardens, and sea urchins. We all explore the surge channels worn into Goat Island's rock ledges, where snails and wracks cling to rock surfaces, and fishes dart in swift flashes of colour.

Hours pass. Vilis and I notice that Dainis's lips have turned blue, so we all return to the beach. Jānis and I continue to snorkel while Dainis and Vilis sit on a grassy slope shaded by wide-crowned *pōhutukawa* trees. An hour later, I'm puckered into goose bumps, yet still Jānis swims with the fishes. Finally, Vilis and I convince him to join us high on the slope above the beach in the sun's soothing warmth. Snorkelling has four new converts.

January 20

A CUCUMBER sails over the garden fence. Vilis catches it neatly. He's standing beside our picnic table in Sheepworld Campground in Dome Valley, north of Goat Island Marine Reserve and its snorkelling hotspot.

"Did you see the wild goats up on the hill?" The campground owner calls out from his garden. His face is shaded by a wide hat as he points at two white goats and a black goat high on the logged hillside across the highway.

We stare groggily at the goats, exhausted after a poor sleep all around. I mention a peculiar, crazy-laughing bird call of last evening.

"Oh, that was a kookaburra [an Australian introduction]," the owner tells me. "There's one fellow that hangs around here."

We breakfast at a table overhung by passionfruits dangling from vines on a trellis. Banana trees entice us to the garden fence, and the scent of wild mint is sharp and clean in the air. Eastern rosellas flit among trees and tree ferns in a woodland at the campground's edge.

After breakfast, we drive north through a collage of forested slopes and grazed hills. When planning our vacation, I reamed off a list of potential adventures and destinations, and each of us chose something special. Tiritiri Mātangi was my choice, and we all thought snorkelling might be fun. Jānis wanted caves, so soon after entering Northland, New Zealand's most northern region, we turn off the main highway and drive to Waipū Caves, west of the small town of Waipū.

Somewhat unexpected, we discover the caves are in a pasture.

Apparently, the limestone karst (a kind of topography formed when soluble limestone dissolves) beneath the paddock is riddled with sinkholes, underground streams, and caverns. At the caves' entrance, swallows hunt flies, and the air holds the peculiar and pervasive scent of onions. Light from one cave entrance beams into a low-ceilinged cavern and reveals wet beige walls, a floor-to-ceiling column of rock, a few stalagmites, and stalactites dripping water into a pool.

Sticky red mud sucks at our rubber boots and smears our hands and clothes as we follow a rock wall into the cave's dark depths. Eerie silence surrounds us, broken only by the sound of water dripping into the pool and the murmur of a shallow stream draining it.

We scramble up onto rock benches and drop down onto stone and mud below. Beside us, water trickles down the cave walls. Huge, rough stalactites hang from the rocky ceiling like teats dripping moisture from massive udders. In the dim light provided by our two small torches and a candle lantern, we see other caves branching off from the one we're in. Vilis twice collides with stalactites, knocking his head. We wish we had more light, and Vilis and I continually call to Dainis, who's so nimble he effortlessly forges ahead, to slow down so we can monitor his safety. In the cave's black depths, multiple passages beckon. Thin, pointed stalactites needle down from ceilings. Glow-worms shine like minute blue stars in soaring caverns of darkness.

After we exit the underground caverns, Jānis comments, "Caves are more interesting and confusing than I expected."

"Yes, they are," I agree, glad that we completed our exploration without any injuries other than Vilis's sore head.

Behind Jānis, a rat runs between boulders. Despite all the rat tracks we collected in Tongariro Forest, this is the first live rat we've seen in New Zealand. It puts a body to what was otherwise only animal sign, and I can only imagine how many others like it roam the landscape.

North beyond Whangārei, the highway meanders through lush agricultural land where dairy herds graze in verdant pastures. Red-flowering shrub roses bookend rows of grapes in a vineyard. Signs greet us: THE FAR NORTH DISTRICT; WELCOME TO THE REALLY FAR NORTH. Houses are modest, and some are run down.

"The farms certainly aren't as manicured as those around Christchurch," I tell Vilis, envisioning that region's hedge-bordered pastures and modern, metal-roofed homes. "There's a laid-back feeling here."

He agrees. "Those Canterbury farmers wouldn't be seen on a farm the likes of these."

January 21

YESTERDAY AFTERNOON, our old Ford Sierra station wagon squeaked and squealed its way to Kaitaia. Vilis steered it into a parking lot and pulled out his AA card to summon roadside assistance. Now, at 11:00 a.m., and with repairs made to a wheel, we drive north on Aupouri Peninsula, heading for Cape Rēinga at New Zealand's northern tip. This is Vilis's "must see" on our vacation.

Pastures patched with thickets of *mānuka* dip and rise on pale green swales over beige and red soils. In the west, sand dunes climb against the sky, and in the east, white beaches touch blue ocean. Vivid orange- and red-flowering cannas grow in roadside ditches, and crates of deep green avocadoes stand piled at a roadside vegetable stand. Dead possums with light brown, dark brown, or black fur litter the highway.

I read our guidebook and inform Vilis and the boys that this narrow finger of land is known to the Māori as Te Hiku-o-te-Ika, "The Tail of the Fish."[51] At the peninsula's north end, the car growls up a narrow gravel road to a lookout and lighthouse at Cape Rēinga.

Atop the cape, signs on a post point to major cities of the world, one citing the distance to Vancouver as 6 229 nautical miles or 11 434 kilometres. Cliffs edge the cape and drop to a broad sweep of sand broken by a headland's rocky arm reaching into the ocean. *Pōhutukawa*, also called New Zealand Christmas trees because of their red balls of flowers, raise broad canopies of leaves to the sea air. Flocks of gulls squabble on the ground and dive from the air to pluck food from tourists' upraised fingers.

Offshore, beyond the landmass that has held them apart for a thousand miles, the Tasman Sea and Pacific Ocean swirl and churn into each other's embrace. Clouds paint blue reflections on the watery turmoil, and small islands string across it like the plated back of a sea dragon, forever waiting to capture departed Māori souls or ferry them to their ancestral homeland. It's said that those souls climb down the rocky headland and drop from the roots of an ancient *pōhutukawa*, which we can see as a tiny silhouette, into the Ocean of Kiwa to make their way back to Hawaiki.[52] Beyond the islands lies only the open immensity of the Pacific. It's not surprising that New Zealand remained unpopulated by humans for so long.

South of the cape, short, thin grasses and stunted *mānuka* grow on dry, impoverished soil. Wild turkeys ramble through pastures. Cicadas buzz like power lines as we pass pine plantations, yet when we drive past stands of *mānuka*, we hear only silence.

As we near Kaitaia, the Bomb's engine begins to sputter. In town, Vilis again calls on AA for emergency repairs, this time to replace damaged spark plug wires. Then we erect our tent in a campground at the south end of Ninety Mile Beach, which is actually sixty-four miles long, according to my guidebook.[53]

When camp chores are done, Vilis and Jānis stash their sneakers atop a sand dune that's one of a rolling expanse of dunes that edge Ninety Mile Beach. Then we walk the sand bordering the Tasman Sea. Māori spirits are said to travel this beach to the ancient tree at Cape Rēinga. The Dutch explorer Abel Tasman, routed twice by the Māori, bestowed the name Cape Maria van Diemen to a volcanic outcrop beyond the beach's north end before he left the island dwellers to their isolated land three and a half centuries ago.[54]

JĀNIS AT NINETY MILE BEACH

At the sea's edge, waves paint the sand into patterns of upside-down feathered wings of great birds, or of hooded creatures with arms extended and dripping the tatters of torn cloaks. We watch clams retreat into the sand at our approach and study Portuguese man-o-wars stranded far from water. The buoyant jellyfishes' bodies and sails shine iridescent blue and purple, and their indigo tentacles stretch a metre long. Dainis inadvertently contacts a tentacle and feels a stinging in the second toe of his left foot. That toe subsequently turns red and hard as a result of the venom injected by the cnidarian's nematocyst, a stinging cell that contains a coiled, barbed attack device, triggered by physical contact.

Dainis's injury doesn't slow him down, and he and Jānis race across the sand and splash through shallow water. Then we all wade in the balmy Tasman Sea. In oncoming dusk, Jānis's figure is a black silhouette against molten silver waves and ripples.

Daylight fades as we return to the sand-dune crevice where Vilis and Jānis stashed their sneakers, only to discover that their footwear isn't where they left it. The theft dismays us. Back at camp, Vilis and Jānis pull on rubber boots stained with the red mud of Waipū Caves.

January 22

AS WE drive south from Kaitaia, where we bought new sneakers for Vilis and Jānis, Dainis asks, "You know how Josephine and Silas said they didn't want to come back from Norway?" He's referring to the children of a zoologist friend whose family spent a year in Norway.

"Yes," Vilis replies.

"Well, I'm starting to like New Zealand, but I miss some things."

Jānis shakes his head. "The longer we stay, the more I miss Canada." His voice sounds forlorn.

Dainis says, "I miss my room, my friends, and the big box of LEGO."

While the boys reminisce about home and Canadian friends, we drive past a roadside cart filled with watermelons and, farther south, past angular hills richly covered with *mānuka* and other trees that comprise Herekino Forest. East of Herekino town, thicket-patched pastures look invitingly cool and rich. Vilis nods to them. "I like this area. It has a backcountry feel. It's not manicured."

Our destination today is Waipoua and its forest of giant *kauri*. "I want to see the place with the big trees," Dainis said when we were planning our vacation, so today is his day for something special. One of those trees is known as Tāne Mahuta, "Lord of the Forest," and is the largest living *kauri*.

Near Kohukohu, mangroves grow in tidal mudflats, their pneumatophores (breathing roots) spiking up through the mud. In the distance, Hokianga Harbour splays blue fingers almost halfway across the northern neck of North Island. From Rangiora, we cross the harbour on a ferry to Rawene and drive south toward Waipoua.

When a harrier cruises low in front of the car, the unexpected close-up of the aerial predator flicks on a light bulb in my mind. After mulling over an idea for a few minutes, I tell Vilis, "I have a theory about why New Zealanders seem to be such thrill seekers."

My husband looks at me in surprise. "Okay. What's your theory?"

"It's because there are no large, dangerous carnivores in this country."

"Explain."

"Well, if there were grizzlies that could eat you back in those hills, New Zealanders wouldn't need to go bungy jumping and jet boating and whatever. They'd get all the adrenaline rush they'd need just by going hiking."

He's sceptical. "Maybe."

I expand on my theory. "This is a benign country, in terms of wildlife. The biggest predatory bird is the harrier, and there are no large, meat-eating mammals, no poisonous snakes, and only one poisonous spider. Maybe there are some sharks and jellyfish offshore, but generally, this country is pretty safe. That makes it a great place to bring children and explore without worrying about being attacked by something, but there's no danger to get the adrenaline pumping. So, New Zealanders *invent* danger."

Vilis laughs. "Could be."

The understory of Waipoua Forest is unlike that of any other New Zealand forest we've encountered. It's dense and cluttered with tall, curving *kauri* grasses, *kiekie* vines, shrubs, perching lilies, and spindly grass trees (*neinei*) with tufts of grass-like leaves. Thick, cylindrical boles of mature *kauri* rise through the understory, unbranched and unencumbered by vines, like massive columns supporting the roof of the sky.

Through a break in the shrubs and tree ferns, we spot Tāne Mahuta. The gigantic *kauri's* trunk, with a girth of thirteen metres, is like the grey leathery leg of a sauropod dinosaur towering above the earth. Framed by fronds and leaves, Tāne Mahuta's trunk and branches rise fifty metres into the air. Its leaf canopy is thin, yet some of the *kauri's* branches are thicker than the trunks of trees around us. A Department of Conservation interpretive display states:

> YOU ARE IN THE PRESENCE OF ONE OF THE MOST ANCIENT OF TREES. IN MAORI COSMOLOGY, TANE IS THE SON OF RANGINUI THE SKY FATHER AND PAPATUANUKU THE EARTH MOTHER. TANE TORE HIS PARENTS APART, BREAKING THEIR PRIMAL EMBRACE, TO BRING LIGHT, SPACE AND AIR AND ALLOWING LIFE TO FLOURISH. TANE IS THE LIFE GIVER – ALL LIVING CREATURES ARE HIS CHILDREN.[55]

We sit on a bench and stare, awestruck, at this relic of New

THIS DARK SHELTERING FOREST

Zealand's ancient forests. The display also informs us that Tāne Mahuta may have sprouted from a seed during the time when Christ walked on the earth.

CAMP IN WAIPOUA FOREST

After we leave the gigantic tree, we set up our tent in a campground at the edge of Waipoua Forest. Then we hike to a look-off with a panoramic view of the surrounding hilly, rain-shrouded landscape. As we begin the downhill tramp from the lookout, I'm caught by an insane impulse. "Let's run!"

"Yeah!" Dainis shouts.

We whoop with laughter and bolt into action. In misting rain, the four of us dash down a narrow track through a forest of giant *kauri*, our hearts leaping with the thrill of treading among them.

DURING THE evening, rain sings softly against the tent while Vilis reads more from Elsie Locke's *A Canoe in the Mist*. This gentle night of our reality is a pleasant contrast to the stark reality of June 10,

1886, when Tarawera – the three-cusped volcanic peak we saw to the north of Lake Taupō from our vantage point of the Tongariro Alpine Crossing – erupted eleven days after the *waka wairua* (ghost canoe) was seen by boat tourists and a guide. That eruption destroyed the Pink and White Terraces and buried two Māori villages.

Dainis and Jānis don't fidget, their faces sober as Vilis reads of tourists and locals who were crushed under the weight of collapsing buildings or suffocated in mud. Survivors were forced out into a howling, sulphurous wind that pelted them with mud and stones blasted into the sky when the mountain split wide open and heaved its fiery guts into the night.[56]

More-pork. More-pork. And the owl's call returns my family to the safety of our here and now.

January 23

SOUTH OF Waipoua Forest, the broad, murky Wairoa River parallels the highway through a flat agricultural landscape of dairy pastures and fields of corn and *kūmara*, the sweet potato Māori explorers brought to this land a thousand years ago. Vilis glances at the waterway. "It's nothing like those big, braided rivers we see on the South Island."

Clumps of pampas grass edge the roadsides. Forested Tokatoka Peak is an anomaly that juts up from the riverside plains. En route to Ōwhango, we angle eastward across the top of splayed fingers of rivers that empty into the Tasman Sea. Then we swing south to Ōrewa, where warm Pacific winds once again caress us and the boys collect *kauri* gum from the trunks of young trees growing in Alice Eaves Scenic Reserve.

Yesterday, in the Waipoua Forest Visitor Centre, we learned that Māori used *kauri* gum for starting fires (this is the attraction for the boys) to supply heat and light. Māori also used the soot from burned gum to make tattoo pigments. Interpretive displays informed us that Pākehā used the gum as an ingredient in varnishes, paints, and linoleum, making it Auckland's biggest export during the 1880s and '90s.

South of Auckland, sun-bleached hills mound against hazy blue sky. We travel southeast over a dry plain bordered on the east by the Kaimai Range's serrated peaks. In Matamata, we pitch our tent beside a tree-shaded knoll at Opal Springs.

Dark clouds billow over the distant Kaimai Range as we luxuriate in the campground's hot mineral pools. Then we play in its competition-sized swimming pool heated by the geothermal activity of the surrounding landscape. For the first time ever, Dainis spends an entire hour in water without his lips turning blue. And for the first time ever, inspired by snorkelling at Goat Island, I plunge beneath the water again and again and swim open-eyed in shimmering blue warmth.

January 24

WE CELEBRATE a new morning with more pool fun then drive quickly southeast from Matamata through farmland and forest to the lakeside city of Rotorua. We arrive just in time to attend a Māori concert at Te Whakarewarewa Thermal Reserve and New Zealand Māori Arts and Crafts Institute.

Before we're allowed to enter the Rotowhio Marae, or sacred courtyard, a slim, muscular Māori warrior, clad in a flax skirt, brandishes a wooden staff. He ritually intimidates and challenges visitors before offering a fern leaf as a symbolic token, a *wero*, to be accepted as a peace gesture.

Kyle, a young man clad in an orange T-shirt and jeans,

solemnly accepts the peace token on behalf of visitors, my family included. Then we're allowed to enter.

Four other warriors stand on wide steps leading up to the *wharenui* (meeting house) behind the greeting warrior. Four women clad in woven flax dresses with bodices displaying triangular designs of red, black, and white stand in a line among the men. Behind the men and women, the white-walled *wharenui* rises to a peak. Its overhanging roof is supported by a ridgepole and is faced with intricately carved posts and bargeboards painted bright red. That colour signifies *tapu* or sacred, and we're told by our guide that the carved wooden facings represent a welcoming and protecting ancestral embrace.

Cautioned to remove our shoes, out of respect, upon entering the *wharenui*, we take our seats for a concert far different from the classical music we heard presented by the Christchurch Symphony Orchestra in October or the performance of *Cinderella* presented by the Royal New Zealand Ballet in November. Here, the influence of Europe remains half a world away. Flax-clad men and women sing and dance, their eyes opening wide to show the whites, their bodies swaying rhythmically in time to the music. The women's arms and hands move with the fluid grace of streaming water. For the *haka*, the men rush forward, fiercely rolling their eyes and wagging their tongues while they perform this traditional preparation for battle. Stick dances and *poi* dances follow, with performers tossing short and long sticks expertly in the first, and women swinging *poi* (pairs of white fuzzy balls attached to both ends of strings) in precise and intricate patterns in the second. The entire performance is one of power, of grace, of pride.

After the concert, we tour the thermal reserve, where it's clear that no frog ever leapt from such a place as Ngāmōkaiakoko,

"Leaping Frog Mud Pool." Its thick, hot mud pushes upward in grey mounds that burst and spit into the air before collapsing into wet-lipped craters. Nearby geysers blast steam high into the air, their bases adorned with pale terraces of minerals precipitated from condensing steam. We observe other mud pools, steaming craters, a boiling spring of water, and a stone seat too hot to sit on. Interpretive displays inform us that early Māori made good use of the land's thermal features by cooking foods in boiling pools and building winter houses dug into the warm soil. Later, in the Carving School, we observe each precise cut made by a young wood carver at work, shaping part of the traditional culture of Aotearoa.

We leave the reserve and pitch our tent in a campground on the shore of Lake Rotorua, where a mud pit bubbles and steams near our shelter. After supper, Vilis reads more from *A Canoe in the Mist*, and we learn how Pākehā survivors of the Tarawera eruption walked, rode, and were carried away from Te Wairoa and the destruction meted out by the volcano, while the Māori stayed to care for their own.[57] As the boys and I listen, heat seeps through the tent floor. We hear mud-thunder explode into the night, and the sulphurous stench of the mud pit fills the tent with its reek. In a small way, it's as though we're at Te Wairoa, too, and in the night, we toss and turn, trying to escape the heat of the earth.

January 25

IN EARLY morning mist, Lake Rotorua is all white, silver, and black, with a *pūkeko* a dark silhouette standing at the water's edge. Crooked tree branches and the curved necks of black swans paint stark pen-and-ink sketches against the lake's surface. Steam rises from the backyard of a house located next to the campground. In Rotorua itself, a cloud of thick vapour hangs over Kuirau Park, which is another geothermal reserve. The entire landscape appears to be exuding heat and belching hot gas, a fact well employed by New Zealand's electricity suppliers.

> ### New Zealand's Geothermal Energy
> Kiwis have tapped geothermal energy as a commercial power source since the late fifties and opened the world's second geothermal power plant at Wairākei, in 1958. About 13 percent of this country's electricity is supplied by geothermal fields, the largest of which is the Taupō Volcanic Zone that stretches across much of central North Island.[58] The region's past violent volcanic activity has resulted in a thin crust of mudstone over porous rock, notably andesite and rhyolite. While the porous rock layers allow magma-heated water and steam to flow through them, the mudstone traps the heated water and steam beneath a hard cap, forcing it to seek escape through vents and faults. It's at such vents and faults that steam can be collected and piped from well heads to power plants such as Wairākei's.[59]

Vilis steers the car south from Rotorua toward Ōwhango, and we pause twice in unrelenting heat to explore other geothermal features. At Wai-O-Tapu Thermal Wonderland, boiling mud pits resemble grey and black ink pots tossed onto an artist's palette of ochre, orange, and shades of green. Beautiful, deadly Champagne Pool simmers emerald beside its bright orange shore. Blue steam rises from its boiling surface. Lake Ngākoro, and a stream draining it, appear almost neon green. Bridal Falls weeps a veil of pale green tears. Although the forest in the vicinity appears natural, these waters look as though they belong to some fantastical world where a dragon's breath would set Champagne Pool boiling and where unicorns would drink from Bridal Falls.

Farther south, at Craters of the Moon, we walk in scorching sunlight among stinking, steaming craters melted out of the earth's crust by underlying magma. Gas clouds drift up from fumaroles, and vividly coloured mineral deposits stain gashes in steaming hillsides. Massive mud pits boil at the bottom of craters. Jagged rocks within *tawa*. All these have nurtured us.

Ripples dance on the lagoon's surface, bumping and jostling as though celebrating each raindrop. An exposed tree root in the old forest resembles an orange-clawed hand glistening with moisture. Jānis grins and jiggles slim *tawa* and lancewood trunks to shake water onto Vilis and me. In retaliation, Vilis shakes leaf-rain onto him, and Jānis laughingly yells, "Hey!"

I stare up into the forest canopy and watch drops of moisture drip from stout branches. I touch ferns and sweep my fingers through draping *rimu* twigs. The boys have forgotten their hacker-whacker sticks today and tread peacefully through the forest. Vilis bemoans the rain that prevents him from photographing the lush greens and shadowy browns, the earthy beiges and spicy cinnamons. When we return to the station wagon parked near Whakapapa River Bridge – the river flexing murky, brown muscles – I'm clutching a pile of twigs and leaves in my hand.

January 27

NEAR WAIKANAE, only seventy kilometres north of Wellington, another fatal car accident has closed the North Island's main traffic artery. We're shaken by this second fatality on the heels of the one near Tūrangi two days ago. The sky is clear. The road is dry. *What happened?*

We're forced to detour north to Palmerston North and then across the gap between the Tarapua and Ruahine Ranges and south through Masterton. The car's radio reports that a muddy hot spring in Rotorua's Kuirau Park erupted yesterday afternoon, blasting stones, mud, and steam more than a hundred metres into the air. The steam cloud was seen five kilometres away.

Dainis and Jānis groan with disappointment. "Why couldn't it have erupted when we drove past the park?" Dainis asks excitedly.

"Yeah!" Jānis exclaims. "That would have been awesome!"

"And probably dangerous," I add, envisioning mud and rocks flying through the air.

After four hours of additional, unplanned driving under bald sun, we finally creep through the gap between the Rimutaka and Tarapua Ranges – those forested, broken ribs of Te Ika-a-Māui – to the homestretch leading into Wellington. Our ferry is long gone. Fortunately, there's space for the Bomb in the line-up for the next ferry, to leave at 5:30 p.m.

Today, the *Arahura* pitches and yaws over what Jānis describes as "a few real waves." In oncoming darkness, Picton's lights welcome us back to South Island. Too exhausted even to eat, we collapse into motel beds, our North Island adventure over. Beginning tomorrow, five more months of South Island explorations await us.

GLOSSARY

Aotearoa – Māori name for New Zealand; means "Land of the Long White Cloud" or "Land of the Long Daylight"

haka – war dance, with chanting

heketara – tree daisy; large shrub or small tree with oval leaves and clusters of small white flowers

kai – food

kākā – forest parrot

kākāriki – red- or yellow-crowned parakeet

kāmahi – tall tree with serrated leaves and spikes of white blossoms

kānuka – shrub or small tree with stringy bark and small, flat leaves

kauri – tall conifer tree with thick, cylindrical trunk and spherical seed cone; among the world's largest trees

kia ora – hello or thank you

kiekie – climbing vine with tufts of long, narrow leaves

koreke – extinct quail

koromiko – rounded shrub with narrow, willowlike leaves

kōura – crayfish

kūmara – yellow-fleshed sweet potato

mānuka – shrub with small, flat, prickly-tipped leaves and white flowers

mataī – tall conifer tree; recently peeled bark creates rounded red scars on trunk

miro – tall coniferous tree that produces fleshy red seed cones

moa – extinct flightless bird

nīkau – native palm tree

pā – hilltop fortress; stockaded village

Pākehā – European or Caucasian

pāua – abalone

podocarp – coniferous tree that produces a fleshy, berrylike seed cone

poi – ball; also, a tuft of white feathers dangling from the throat of *tūī*

ponga – silver fern

pūkeko – marsh bird with blue-black plumage; swamp hen

rimu – tall conifer tree with weeping twigs

tapu – sacred

tawa – tall hardwood tree with narrow, pointed leaves

toetoe – a large tussock grass with long, rough-edged leaves and creamy flower plumes on long stems

tōtara – conifer tree with stringy bark, flat needles, and fleshy red seed cones

tūī – blackish-brown songbird with two white feather tufts dangling from throat

waka – canoe

waka wairua – ghost canoe

warehou – a South Pacific fish

whēkī – stout tree fern with a thick skirt of dead leaves

REFERENCES

[1] Keith Sinclair. (2000). *A History of New Zealand*. Auckland: Penguin Books. pp. 14, 19, 29-31.

[2] Ministry for Primary Industries *Manatū Ahu Matua*. (Accessed 6-Mar-2015). "Travel and Recreation: Items to Declare." http://www.mpi.govt.nz/travel-and-recreation/arriving-in-new-zealand/items-to-declare/.

[3] Department of Conservation *Te Papa Atawhai*. (Accessed 6-Mar-2015). "Animal Pests – Stoats." http://www.doc.govt.nz/conservation/threats-and-impacts/animal-pests/animal-pests-a-z/stoats/.

[4] Department of Conservation *Te Papa Atawhai*. (Accessed 6-Mar-2015). "Birds – Kiwi." http://www.doc.govt.nz/conservation/native-animals/birds/birds-a-z/kiwi/.

[5] Department of Conservation *Te Papa Atawhai*. (Accessed 4-May-2015). "Common weeds – Russell lupin." http://www.doc.govt.nz/nature/pests-and-threats/common-weeds/russell-lupin/; Q. Paynter, A. H. Gourlay, C. A. Rolando, and M. S. Watt. (Accessed 4-May-2015). "Dispersal of the Scotch broom gall mite *Aceria genistae*: implications for biocontrol." (2012). *New Zealand Plant Protection* 65: 81–84. http://www.nzpps.org/journal/65/nzpp_650810.pdf

[6] Eileen McSaveney. (Accessed 4-May-2015). "Glaciers and glaciation – Retreating ice and the glacier legacy." *Te Ara* – The Encyclopedia of New Zealand, http://www.TeAra.govt.nz/en/glaciers-and-glaciation/4; Wikipedia. (Accessed 4-May-2015) "List of Lakes in New Zealand." http://en.wikipedia.org/wiki/List_of_lakes_in_New_Zealand.

[7] Thomas D. Isern. (2002). "Companions, Stowaways, Imperialists, Invaders: Pests and Weeds in New Zealand." In *Environmental Histories of New Zealand*, edited by Eric Pawson and Tom Brooking. South Melbourne: Oxford University Press. p. 233; Wikipedia. (Accessed 4-May-2015). "Mackenzie Basin." http://en.wikipedia.org/wiki/Mackenzie_Basin.

[8] Isern, p. 237; Wikipedia, http://en.wikipedia.org/wiki/Mackenzie_Basin.

[9] Isern, pp. 237-240; N. L. Forrester, B. Boag, S. R. Moss, S. L. Turner, R. C. Trout, P. J. White, P. J. Hudson and E. A. Gould. (2003). "Long- term survival of New Zealand rabbit hemorrhagic disease virus RNA in wild rabbits, revealed by RT-PCR and phylogenetic analysis." *Journal of General Virology* 84:3079-3086.

[10] Stuff.co.nz. (Accessed 4-May-2015). Matthew Littlewood. "1080 drops for rabbits 'inevitable'." *The Timaru Herald*, (updated 11-Jul-2009). http://www.stuff.co.nz/timaru-herald/news/2584583/1080-drops-for-rabbits-inevitable.

[11] Christchurch City Libraries *Ngā Kete Wānanga-o-Ōtautahi*. (Accessed 4-May-2015). "Ōtamahua – Quail Island." http://my.christchurchcitylibraries.com/ti-kouka-whenua/otamahua/; Black Cat Group. (Accessed 10-Dec-2000). "Quail Island Recreational Reserve." Visitor's information pamphlet.

[12] Paynter, *et. al.* http://www.nzpps.org/journal/65/nzpp_650810.pdf; Wikipedia. (Accessed 4-May-2015). "*Cystisus scoparius*." http://en.wikipedia.org/wiki/Cytisus_scoparius.

[13] Laura Harper, Tony Mudd, and Paul Whitfield. (1998). *New Zealand: The Rough Guide*. London: The Rough Guides. p. 473.

[14] *Ibid*, p. 470.

[15] Judith Bassett, Keith Sinclair, and Marcia Stenson. (1985). *The Story of New Zealand*. Auckland: Reed Methuen. p. 19.

[16] Andrew Crowe. (1998). *Which Native Tree? A Simple Guide to the Identification of New Zealand Native Trees*. Auckland: Penguin Books (NZ) Ltd. pp. 41, 46.

[17] Andrew Crowe. (1994). *Which Native Forest Plant? A Simple Guide to the Identification of New Zealand Native Forest Shrubs, Climbers and Flowers*. Auckland: Penguin Books (NZ) Ltd. p. 38, 51.

[18] Graeme Wynn. (2002). "Destruction Under the Guise of Improvement? The Forest, 1840- 1920." In *Environmental Histories of New Zealand*, edited by Eric Pawson and Tom Brooking. South Melbourne: Oxford University Press. p. 102.

[19] Harper, Mudd, and Whitfield, p. 211.

[20] Wikipedia. (Accessed 4-May-2015). "Owhango." http://en.wikipedia.org/wiki/Owhango.

[21] Department of Conservation *Te Papa Atawhai*. (Accessed 4-May-2015). "Land birds – Kiwi." http://www.doc.govt.nz/nature/native-animals/birds/birds-a-z/kiwi/.

[22] Kay Griffith. (Accessed 4-May-2015). "Stoat Control in New Zealand: A Review." (1999). Wildlife Management Report Number 108, University of Otago, p. 5-11. http://theconservationcompany.co.nz/pdf/stoat%20thesis.pdf.

[23] *Ibid*, pp. 3-4.

[24] Andrea E. Byrom. (Accessed 4-May-2015). "Stoat captures in a year of heavy mountain beech seedfall." (2004). Department of Conservation *Te Papa*

Atawhai. DOC Science Internal Series 163, p. 5. http://www.doc.govt.nz/documents/science-and-technical/dsis163.pdf.

[25] Department of Conservation *Te Papa Atawhai*. (Accessed 4-May-2015). "Tongariro Forest Conservation Area." http://www.doc.govt.nz/parks-and-recreation/places-to-visit/central-north-island/ruapehu-area/tongariro-forest-conservation-area/.

[26] About Travel. (Accessed 4-May-2015). Liam Naden. "Lake Taupo Facts and Figures." http://gonewzealand.about.com/od/Rotorua-Lake-Taupo-Destination/a/Lake-Taupo-Facts-And-Figures.htm.

[27] New Zealand Geothermal Association. (Accessed 5-May-2015). "Geothermal Energy – Geology." http://www.nzgeothermal.org.nz/education/geology.html. (Quoted by kind permission.)

[28] GNS Science *Te Pū Ao*. (Accessed 5-May-2015). Paul Froggatt. "Volcanic Hazards at Taupo Volcanic Centre." (1997). Ministry of Civil Defence. Volcanic hazards information series 7. 26 p. Palmerston North, NZ. http://www.gns.cri.nz/Home/Learning/Science-Topics/Volcanoes/New-Zealand-Volcanoes/Volcano-Geology-and-Hazards/Taupo-Volcanic-Centre-Geology.

[29] *Ibid*; Oregon State University. (Accessed 5-May-2015). "Taupo, New Zealand." http://volcano.oregonstate.edu/vwdocs/volc_images/australia/new_zealand/taupo.html; All Experts. (Accessed 5-May-2015). C. Robert Teszka, Jr. "Geology – Volcanoes – The most destructive volcano." (2005). http://en.allexperts.com/q/Geology-1359/volcano-s.htm.

[30] Department of Conservation *Te Papa Atawhai*. (Accessed 5-May-2015). "Tongariro Forest Conservation Area pest control operation completed." (5 September 2014). http://www.doc.govt.nz/news/media-releases/2014/tongariro-forest-conservation-area-pest-control-operation-completed/.

[31] Eileen McSaveney. (Accessed 5-May-2015). "Glaciers and glaciation – Glaciers in New Zealand." *Te Ara* – the Encyclopedia of New Zealand. http://www.TeAra.govt.nz/en/glaciers-and-glaciation/page-1.

[32] Volcano Discovery. (Accessed 5-May-2015). "Ruapehu volcano (New Zealand): crater lake temperature near peak cycle." (February 5, 2015). http://www.volcanodiscovery.com/ruapehu/news/50902/Ruapehu-volcano-New-Zealand-crater-lake-temperature-near-peak-of-heating-cycle.html

[33] George Gibbs. (Accessed 5-May-2015). "Glow-worms – New Zealand's glow-worms." *Te Ara* – the Encyclopedia of New Zealand. http://www.TeAra.govt.nz/en/glow-worms/page-1.

[34] *Ibid*.

[35] Department of Conservation *Te Papa Atawhai*. (1999). "Tongariro National Park World Heritage Information Package." pp. 1, 3.

[36] Keith Sinclair. (2000 revised edition). *A History of New Zealand*. Auckland: Penguin Books. pp. 116-117. (Quoted by kind permission.)

[37] Department of Conservation, *Te Papa Atawhai*. (Accessed 5-May-2015). "Ohakune area tramping tracks." http://www.doc.govt.nz/parks-and-recreation/tracks-and-walks/central-north-island/ruapehu/ohakune-area-tramping-tracks/.

[38] Department of Conservation, *Te Papa Atawhai*. (Accessed 5-May-2015). "Central North Island volcanoes." http://www.doc.govt.nz/parks-and-recreation/places-to-go/central-north-island/places/tongariro-national-park/about-tongariro-national-park/central-north-island-volcanoes/.

[39] *Ibid.*

[40] Eileen McSaveney, Carol Stewart and Graham Leonard. (Accessed 5-May-2015). "Historic volcanic activity – Tongariro and Ngāuruhoe." *Te Ara* – the Encyclopedia of New Zealand. http://www.TeAra.govt.nz/en/historic-volcanic-activity/page-3.

[41] Department of Conservation, *Te Papa Atawhai*. (Accessed 5-May-2015). "Central North Island volcanoes." http://www.doc.govt.nz/parks-and-recreation/places-to-go/central-north-island/places/tongariro-national-park/about-tongariro-national-park/central-north-island-volcanoes/.

[42] Department of Conservation *Te Papa Atawhai*. (1999). "The Tongariro Crossing." Tongariro/Taupo Conservancy. Visitor's information leaflet.

[43] *Ibid.*

[44] Phyllis Johnston. (1982). *Black Boots and Buttonhooks*. Wellington: Price Milburn. p. 105.

[45] Elsie Locke. (1984). *A Canoe in the Mist*. London: Jonathan Cape Ltd. pp. 27-54.

[46] Carleton University, Hooper Museum (Ottawa). (Accessed 5-May-2015). "How the Kiwi Lost His Wings." http://hoopermuseum.earthsci.carleton.ca/flightless/losewing.htm.

[47] Debra Vrana. (Accessed 5-May-2015). "A Pox upon the Kauri."*Smithsonian Magazine*, October 2007, pp. 4-5. http://www.smithsonianmag.com/arts-culture/a-pox-upon-the-kauri-172941380/; Gretel Boswijk. (Accessed 5-May-2015). "A History of Kauri." In *Australia and New Zealand Forest Histories: Auraucarian Forests*. (2005) Edited by J. Dargavel. Australian Forest History Society Inc. Occasional Publication No. 2. Kingston. pp. 19-26. http://environmentalhistory-au-nz.org/links/publications/anzfh/anzfh2boswijk.pdf; Atholl Anderson. (2002). "A Fragile Plenty: Pre-European Māori and the New Zealand Environment." In *Environmental Histories of New Zealand*, edited by Eric

Pawson and Tom Brooking. South Melbourne: Oxford University Press. p. 31; Evelyn Stokes. (2002). "Contesting Resources – Māori, Pākehā, and a Tenurial Revolution." In *Environmental Histories of New Zealand*. pp. 42-43; Wynn, pp. 105-108.

[48] Doug Armstrong. (Accessed 5-May-2015). "Tiritiri Matangi Island Restoration Programme." (1999). Massey University, Reintroduction Specialist Group Oceania Section. http://www.massey.ac.nz/~darmstro/tiri.htm; Tiritiri Matangi Open Sanctuary. (Accessed 5-May-2015). "Habitat restoration." http://www.tiritirimatangi.org.nz/habitat.

[49] Hugh Robertson and Barrie Heather. (1999). *The Hand Guide to the Birds of New Zealand*. Auckland: Penguin Books. p. 156.

[50] *Ibid*; Tiritiri Matangi Open Sanctuary. (Accessed 5-May-2015). "Details of the Tiritiri takahe." http://www.tiritirimatangi.org.nz/takahe-on-tiri.

[51] Harper, Mudd, and Whitfield, p. 176.

[52] Sinclair, p. 22.

[53] Harper, Mudd, and Whitfield, p. 176.

[54] Harper, Mudd, and Whitfield, p. 176; Bassett, Sinclair, and Stenson, p. 19.

[55] Department of Conservation *Te Papa Atawhai*. Interpretive sign in Waipoua Forest. (Quoted by kind permission.)

[56] Locke, pp. 90-179.

[57] Locke, pp. 155-188.

[58] New Zealand Geothermal Association. (Accessed 5-May-2015). "Geothermal Energy – Geothermal Energy & Electricity Generation." http://www.nzgeothermal.org.nz/elec_geo.html.

[59] New Zealand Geothermal Association. (Accessed 5-May-2015). "Geothermal Energy – Geology." http://www.nzgeothermal.org.nz/education/geology.html.

INDEX

Alice Eaves Scenic Reserve, 155, 170
Aotearoa, 1, 68, 173, 179
Aupouri Peninsula, 163
Banks Peninsula, 16, 19, 45
Blyth Track, 140, 141
Cape Rēinga, 163
cave, 39, 40, 162
    Waipū Caves, 161
Cook Strait, 43
Craters of the Moon, 174, 175
explorers
    Cook, James, 43
    Tasman, Abel, 1, 43, 165
glaciated lakes, 6
glow worm, 83, 115, 162
haka, 172, 179
Hawaiki, 164
history
    environmental, 55, 62, 156
    Kaikōura, 29
    Lake Taupō, 68
    Māori, 118, 170, 171, 173
    Quail Island, 19
    Tarawera eruption, 170, 173
    Te Wairoa, 151
invasive species
    possum, 122
    rabbit, 7, 8, 55
    rat, 122, 162
    stoat, 2, 5, 6, 55, 56, 59, 75, 122
Kaikōura, 25, 28, 29, 41
    Peninsula, 25
    Seaward Kaikōura Range, 26, 28, 41
Kākahi, 83, 115
kiwi, 2, 6, 52, 55, 63, 75, 153, 154
Kuratau River, 69
Lake Rotopounamu, 70
Lake Rotorua, 173
Lake Tarawera, 151
Lake Taupō, 66, 67, 68, 145
Lincoln, 9, 15
Lindis Pass Scenic Reserve, 6
Lindis Valley, 6
Locke, Elsie, 151, 169
Lyttelton, 16
    Harbour, 16, 18

Mackenzie Basin, 7, 8
Mangawhero Forest, 45
mistletoe, 122
Mounds of the Murimoto Formation, 118
New Zealand forest structure, 46
Ninety Mile Beach, 164, 165
Ohau Point, 41
Ōhinetonga
    Lagoon, 98, 123, 132
    Loop Track, 81
    Scenic Reserve, 47, 123, 176
Ōruanui eruption, 68, 117
Ōwhango, 47, 49, 63
Ōwhango Black 2000, 87
Peninsula Walkway, 26, 30
Point Kean, 31, 35
Quail Island, 16, 18, 19
Rotorua, 171, 173, 177
seal, southern fur, 31, 35, 39, 41
Silica Rapids Track, 122
Sinclair, Keith, 118
snorkelling
    Goat Island Marine Reserve, 159
takahē, 157, 158
Tāne Mahuta, 153, 154, 167, 168, 169

Taranaki Falls, 101
    Track, 100
Taumarunui, 48, 62, 83, 84, 113, 131
Taupō eruption, 68
Te Heuheu Tūkino IV, 118, 141
Te Whakarewarewa Thermal Reserve and New Zealand Māori Arts and Crafts Institute, 171
Tiritiri Mātangi, 156, 157, 158, 159
Tongariro
    Alpine Crossing, 140, 141, 145
    Forest, 57, 62, 65, 72, 92, 129
    Forest Conservation Area, 47, 63, 75
    National Park, 99, 100, 117, 122, 128
volcano, 65, 99, 123
    Akaroa, 16
    Lyttelton, 16
    Ngāuruhoe, 65, 118, 144
    Ruapehu, 65, 68, 99, 117, 118, 122
    Taranaki, 66, 142
    Tarawera, 170, 173

Tongariro, 65, 117, 118, 142, 144
Wai-O-Tapu Thermal Wonderland, 174
Waipoua Forest, 168
Wanganui, 44
Wellington, 9, 44, 52
Whakapapa, 99, 100
  Bush Road, 47
  River, 47, 50
  Ski Field, 123
Whakapapanui Track, 128

Made in the USA
Charleston, SC
28 May 2015